Foreward and Acknowledgments:

This is a real book by a real startup manufacturing entrepreneur. The book is not the result of an intellectual brainstorming session among so-called experts who have no ground experience. Rather, this is a true story comprising of the true events in the startup journey of a manufacturing entrepreneur in India. Therefore, there are no views. There are only facts. The challenges faced by a manufacturing startup entrepreneur are documented in this book. The book looks at the 'Make in India' program from a startup entrepreneur's perspective. The book also suggests solutions to make Indian manufacturing globally competitive.

As I started to write this manufacturing journey, a journey that is mostly frustrated and helpless, several thoughts crossed my mind as to how things could have been quicker and better for the manufacturing industry as a whole with little support from various stakeholders at a policy level. The various stakeholders include government, policymakers, various manufacturing industry bodies, financial lenders.

Thanks to Sumit who encouraged me to write this book. Without his encouraging words, this book wouldn't have been possible. Thanks also to each and everyone who is part of this book.

Common Terms Used:

Mold

Mold or Mould is a rigid frame that is at the heart of any manufacturing business. Be it Fast Moving Electrical Goods manufacturing, auto manufacturing, household goods manufacturing, textile manufacturing, toy manufacturing, all kinds of manufacturing businesses require a mold to make repeatable pieces in the production line.

Die

Like a Mold, a Die is a rigid tool or frame that is used to make repeatable finished pieces in the production line.

Babu

The central government or state governments public servants or bureaucrats involved in making and implementing policies including economic policies.

Tool-room

A Tool-room is everything related to tools and Dies/Molds. The Tool-room is different from a production line. In a Tool-room, tools and Molds/Dies are developed. Whereas in a production line, repeatable pieces are made using the tools, Molds/Dies.

Prototype

A prototype is a first sample, model, or release of a product that is built to test how the final saleable product will appear, how the final saleable product will be fitted, how the

1

final saleable product will function. After evaluating the prototype, the entrepreneur or management team decides whether to make changes in the final saleable product or not.

Top-down manufacturing

A manufacturing approach wherein a large business sets up a manufacturing facility to manufacture products. The products could be anything such as cars, washing machines, mobile phones, etc. Once this large business sets up a manufacturing facility, the ancillary units come up to supply different parts to this large manufacturing business. For example, Maruti started car manufacturing in Gurgaon. To support Maruti, ancillary units supplying different parts such as screws/nuts, brake systems, clutches, pistons, etc. came up in Gurgaon. The whole manufacturing ecosystem evolved once Maruti started operations in Gurgaon. This is known as Top-down manufacturing. Top-down manufacturing can also be termed as capital intensive manufacturing. Automation has taken over this kind of manufacturing. Therefore, we keep hearing about high productivity but lack of new job generation in this kind of manufacturing.

Bottom-up manufacturing

A manufacturing approach wherein a product idea evolves in an entrepreneur's mind. The entrepreneur tests the idea and decides to manufacture the products. This idea could be about manufacturing any products such as toys, agarbatti, chappals, new innovative products, etc. A big company such as Maruti, Samsung, LG won't be producing these items. Only an entrepreneur with an idea can take the plunge and manufacture these products. Bottom-up manufacturing can also be termed as labor-intensive manufacturing. This is where most of the manufacturing jobs are created.

Manufacturing society

Just like a housing society wherein thousands of apartment owners live, in a manufacturing society thousands of space owners manufacture all kinds of products. With the adoption of a manufacturing society concept, the process of getting approvals becomes faster and economies of scale can be achieved.

Mosquiter

Mosquiter is a product that we as a startup have built. It is an exhaust fan that also catches & kills mosquitoes. Here is an image of our manufactured product.

Front Cover

Back Cover

Fan

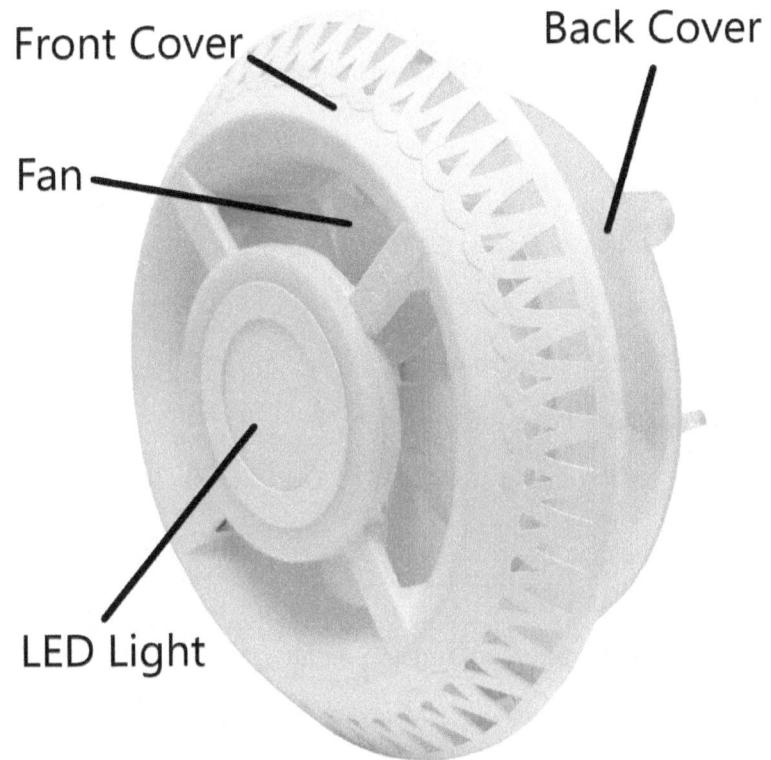

LED Light

Contents

Chapter 1

It all starts with an Idea

March 2018, having been unsuccessful in my previous entrepreneurial endeavors on online real estate platforms, I was sitting in my drawing room in a pensive mood. With nothing to do, I picked up the daily newspaper and an article on 'Manufacturing' caught my eye. By this time, I had lost interest in reading the editorial section of the newspaper. All I would do is just glance through the news and that's it. An editorial in the newspaper has lost the appeal for me probably because of the biased views of the people writing those articles in the newspaper. But this article on 'Manufacturing' caught my eye and I ended up reading the whole article. And as had been the case with many of these one-sided articles in the editorial section, the writer gloated about how Indian manufacturing is going to transform; how new jobs are going to be created; how GDP will grow fast; how per capita income is set to rise in India.

I wondered if the 'Manufacturing' sector is going to transform in India, then, how the hell India's trade deficit with China is burgeoning year after year.

I also wondered if the 'Manufacturing' sector is transforming, then, why traders across India are buying goods from China and selling in India. From simple items like 'Chappal' to 'Agarbatti' to 'Diwali Lights' to 'Holi Pichkaris' to 'Toys' to electrical items such as 'switches' to 'fans' to 'LED' to even our 'Gods' sculptures' are being sourced from China and sold in India. Why is this happening? Surely, big manufacturing companies like

Samsung, LG, Maruti, etc. won't manufacture these simple items. These simple items would have to be produced by small scale entrepreneurs. I wondered, why aren't small scale entrepreneurs doing it? What stops them from producing these simple items in India? Why are they all going to China and flooding Indian markets with Chinese goods? I had no answers to those questions.

India Imports from China (US $ Billion), India Exports to China (US $ Billion) and Trade Deficit (US $ Billion)

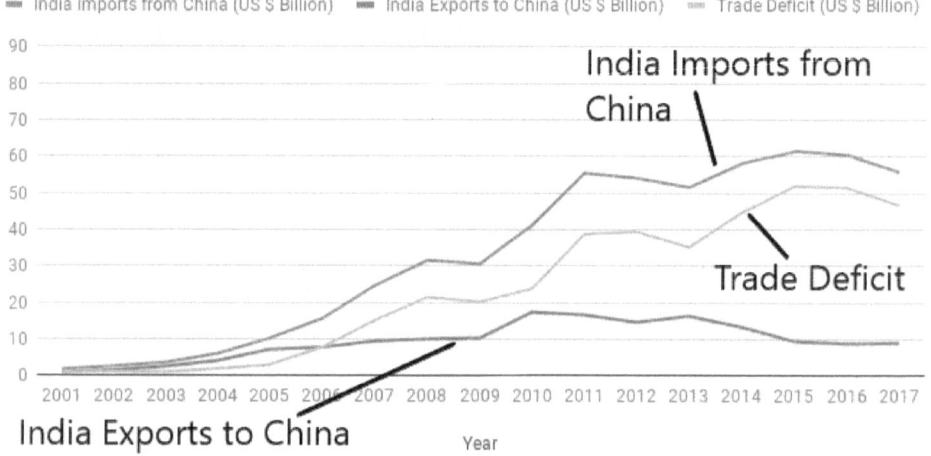

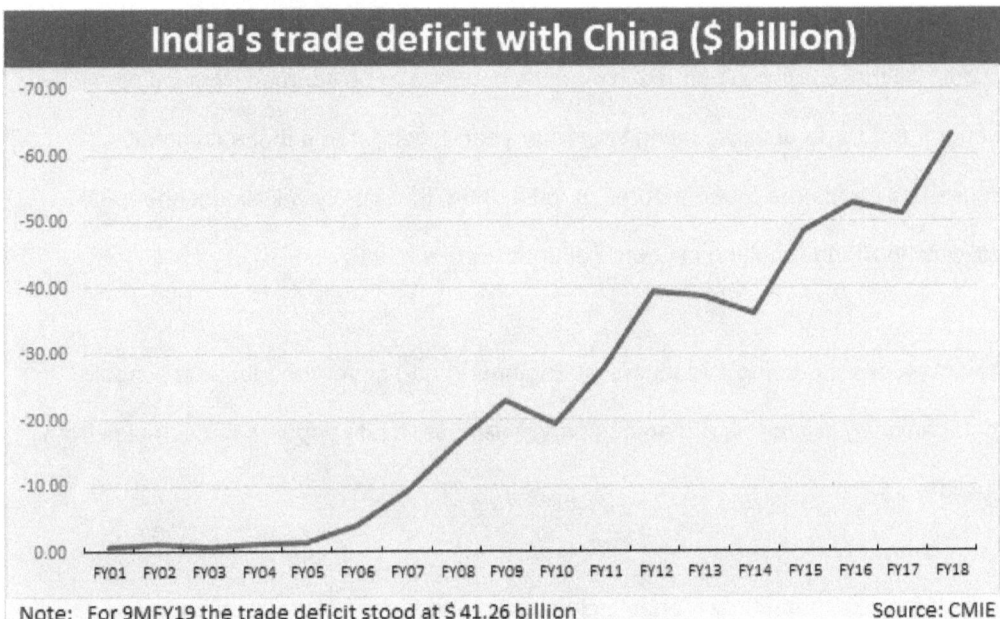

India's trade deficit with China ($ billion)

Note: For 9MFY19 the trade deficit stood at $ 41.26 billion   Source: CMIE

I kept wondering why didn't the writer of that article highlighted the reasons behind Indian entrepreneurs going to China and buying simple manufactured goods from there and selling in India. I wondered why the writer just focused on big manufacturing companies such as Samsung, LG, Maruti and how these companies are going to create jobs in India. Surely, these big companies won't be manufacturing 'Chappals', 'Agarbatti', 'Diwali Lights', 'Holi Pichkaris', 'LED', 'Switches', etc. So, who the hell is going to produce these simple items in India?

The author of that article also gloated upon 'Defence Manufacturing in India'. Again, these are all high tech manufacturing products, but what about the low tech or simple manufacturing items that are consumed by households across India on a daily basis?

The author of that article simply didn't dwell on these simple yet common household goods. All these common household goods continue to be sourced from China. No wonder, our trade deficit is rising year after year. I wondered if these common household goods are manufactured in India, then, that surely will reduce the trade deficit with China resulting in Crores of Jobs across India.

Anyways, despite being a Mechanical Engineer, I had never thought deeply about manufacturing or starting a manufacturing business. It just appears too complex from outside.

In fact, I thought about my friends including college friends & previous company colleagues, and none of them were working in manufacturing companies except an odd one or two. Most of the people in my network were all employed in the Information Technology sector. And many of them were living abroad. We never discussed or talked about manufacturing or manufacturing products. We would always talk about ideas related to starting an online business such as carpooling, online grocery, other Apps. But never once did we talk about manufacturing a product in India. Never. I wondered, is this the reason for not hearing about manufacturing entrepreneurs in India? People are just not interested in starting a manufacturing business in India? They are happy to become traders. Bring goods from China and sell them in India.

The author of that article on 'Manufacturing' didn't dwell on these issues either.

The evening was taking its full effect, and suddenly a deluge of mosquitoes started to piss me off. March is the month when winter gives way to spring, and the temperature is ideal for mosquitoes to breed and become a nuisance in every household.

But till March 2018, I hadn't thought of mosquitoes as a nuisance. I was living in Faridabad and even though mosquitoes were present there as well, the problem was partially remedied by the use of prevailing solutions such as Mosquito repellent, Mosquito net, Mosquito coils, etc. However, in October 2017, I had moved to Noida, and in March 2018, I witnessed this large scale stream of mosquitoes that I had never seen before. The problem was so massive that Mosquito repellent, Mosquito coils, or Mosquito nets were rendered ineffective. I felt like taking a vacuum cleaner and suck all these blood-sucking annoying mosquitoes. There it is, an organic idea had gripped my mind. An idea worth exploring. An idea about how to solve the Mosquito problem for me. I wasn't even bothered about making it a mass scale idea. I knew from my past entrepreneurial experiences that having an idea is one thing and executing it on a larger scale is another thing. So, I just focused on solving the Mosquito problem for my house.

My mechanical engineering studies came in handy at this time. I began to conceptualize the product in my mind. The thoughts remained with me for 2-3 days and grew stronger and stronger by the day. Generally, an entrepreneurial mind is always looking for ideas, and some of those ideas peter down after the euphoria of initial 2-3 days or a week. That petering down of ideas is very important for an entrepreneur. If an idea can't occupy the entrepreneur's mind for long enough, then, the idea itself is not worth investing your time, money, and energy into it.

However, this Mosquito idea persisted with me. I started to read my engineering textbooks about suction and how to accomplish it. I also started to look at various signals that mosquitoes use to prey on humans. After a thoughtful 2-3 weeks, I decided to make a prototype or a product for my home.

I also contacted my Mama (Distant Uncle). I called him and started discussing the manufacturing industry. I didn't even talk about mosquitoes with him. Despite understanding that 'having an idea is one thing and executing it on a larger scale is another', I still resisted sharing my 'Mosquito' idea with my Mama (Distant Uncle). The next day, I called him again. This time, he was busy and hung up the phone saying he will call me later. That 'later' came 2 days later though.

He called me in the morning, yea, Sachin, we were discussing manufacturing business and all. What were you saying?
I said I have been doing 'Machine Learning' for 4-5 months and I thought of building a robotic vacuum cleaner. This robotic vacuum cleaner will operate on the basis of data collected over a period of time.

Well, that was my way of not sharing my original 'Mosquito' idea. I was only concerned with the vacuum process and how it can be utilized to suck mosquitoes. More importantly, I wanted to find out about motor manufacturers, blades manufacturers, etc. I was least interested in vacuum cleaners. However, Mama started explaining to me the challenges that will be faced while attempting such a product (robotic vacuum cleaner). During this discussion, he himself started narrating his own 'Mosquito' idea that he had thought of 3-4 years ago. I was like, what, really? I didn't say this to him but wondered why didn't he actually do it then? Well, we decided to talk again 2-3 days later.

I called him now, 2-3 days later, and this time, we solely discussed the 'Mosquito idea'. I was asking, why didn't he attempt it? I got the sense that he didn't attempt it because of various reasons such as existing work pressure, lack of marketing know-how, and the effectiveness of the product that he had envisioned in his mind.

Later, I traveled to his manufacturing facility near Hapur. I was impressed with what I saw. He had invested a good amount of money into setting up a big CNC machine, boiler, cooling tower, and Molds. He was under tremendous pressure to deliver the bottling solutions that he was manufacturing there. For the first time, I came to know about various terminologies such as 'Dana (Plastic Raw material)', and various kinds of this 'Dana'. He also showed me the 2 appliances that he had bought from China to catch mosquitoes.

We discussed possible designs that we can develop for our 'Mosquito' product. The meeting ended and I came back home carrying with me one of his Chinese made 'Mosquito appliance'.

As soon as I came home, I searched for such an appliance on Amazon and Flipkart. It was selling for Rupees 600 apiece. I also wanted to know the sales volume of such a machine, but it was impossible to find out. However, from the rankings on Amazon, I came to realize that the product was not selling well.

I started using this appliance in my home, and it was a disaster. The appliance won't catch mosquitoes at all, at most 2-3 mosquitoes, that too, when all the lights were switched off and we were not inside the house. My family members termed the appliance as 'Kuda (Waste)'.

This machine was using a low power 3 inches fan and small blue LEDs. The LEDs will attract the mosquitoes and a fan will suck them. That simple. However, the results were too bad. Can you imagine the suction created by the 3 inches fan? I could, it was too low. It was not sufficient to pull distant mosquitoes. Moreover, the design of this Chinese made 'Mosquito' appliance was along the lines of a 'Lantern'. In other words, the relative motion of mosquitoes and the suction pressure created by the small fan was perpendicular in nature. Which meant, it was difficult to suck mosquitoes flying at high speed in the horizontal direction, whereas the suction pressure created by the small fan was in the vertically downward direction.

At the same time, the blue LEDs were so small that I wondered how would even mosquitoes detect their wavelengths from the distance. Other than that, this Chinese made appliance used Chinese plastic (cheap plastic body). There was no other research and development in this highly ineffective appliance.

I had thought of and conceptualized a comprehensive solution. A solution that will basically simulate the human body to first attract the mosquitoes and then suck them up with a high airflow low power fan. The fan blades in my plan were different from the normal blades sold in the market.

In my previous job at a software company engineering services department, I had worked on turbine components. Yes, I am a Mechanical Engineer. Therefore, I was aware of the blade angles that can increase airflow without increasing the input power. Increased airflow will mean higher suction pressure without increasing the power input. So, the experience at the software company came in handy. Well, I now feel most experiences come in handy provided you had put in some effort in whatever activity you had performed in the past. Or put it simply, absolute involvement in any activity may come in handy in the future.

I called my Mama after using this Chinese appliance for 2-3 days. Mama was eager to listen to my feedback about this appliance. I uttered 'Kuda'. He started laughing as if to suggest that 'thank god, we are not going to make this appliance and waste our time and money'. I said, no no, we are going to make this product in partnership. But our product will be much more comprehensive.

I started giving him examples of famous entrepreneurs such as Steve Jobs, Google Founders, etc.'. I wanted to convey the point that no matter if the same product had been attempted in the past, the challenge or innovation lies in improving the product. That's what Steve Jobs or Google founders did and did it well. Well, with this Mosquito product, we are not going to get anywhere near Steve Jobs or Google founders. However, the idea was to motivate my Mama to take this plunge with me in the development of a comprehensive Mosquito product.

Mama was excited at first, he said, yea, we will do it, however, 2-3 days down the line, he backed down. Why? The pressure of his existing business and maybe the age as well. I guess it's difficult to be an entrepreneur after 55. I may be wrong, but, that's what I felt with my interaction with him.

Well, I was so convinced by the idea that I wanted to do it. In fact, at first, I wanted to do it alone to retain 100% control in my hands. However, I wanted him to join in because not only he would have brought in money but also he would have provided access to his manufacturing facility. Despite being a mechanical engineer, I was pretty weak in manufacturing. In fact, I had no idea as to how the manufacturing of this Mosquito product will take place. Where will we source the necessary parts from? Where will we get the mold from? Where will we manufacture? Where will we assemble? Where will we do the packaging? And then, finally, market and sell. Lots of work and I said to myself, 'can't be done alone', given that I have no resources, no money (not even 1 Lac Rupee).

I tried to persuade my Mama but all in vain. He had made up his mind not to get involved in this Mosquito product. However, I was excited about building such a product. At the same time, I was aware of the challenges that I will have to face if at all I decided to attempt this product. I visited Mama's manufacturing facility again in order to persuade him. He elaborated on his reasons for not joining in. We had lunch and on my way home, Sumit called me.

Sumit is my long-time buddy. We had known each other since we were born. Well, not exactly from the kindergarten days, but from Class 7 or Class 8. We did schooling together including championing the PCM Class 12 results as well as securing a good rank in regional Government engineering college. Getting into the government regional engineering college meant you end up doing your engineering degree virtually for Free. Yea, the tuition fee and hostel fee used to be so low that even the cost involved in traveling once or twice from home to college was much higher.

However, despite the talent, we did not focus much on studies during engineering. We never came up with ideas or start-up ideas. Maybe the ecosystem at that time was not ripe for startups or new ideas. Somehow we ended up getting an engineering degree by just studying for a night or two before every semester exam.

Post engineering, we pursued our own paths. Sumit got into a Public sector unit and I joined the revolutionary Indian IT sector. Even though I joined the IT sector, I still ended up working in the Mechanical Design field. I worked in the design department for a Gas Turbine Power Plant client. I got the opportunity to learn Computer-Aided Design (CAD) software. Well, that was about our career paths. Sumit and I along with other local school and college friends remained in contact. I did not mind discussing my ideas with Sumit. And believe me, I would have discussed at least 20 or 30 of such ideas with Sumit including my online real estate platform idea.

So, on my way home from Mama's manufacturing facility, Sumit called up.

Hare Krishna, Sumit said.

Well, that's another interesting story as to how a non-vegetarian, alcohol-consuming, and smoking guy became a complete saint.

I said, Hare Krishna.

What's going on? Sumit asked.

Coming back home from Hapur, I said.

Hapur? What the hell were you doing in Hapur? Sumit asked again.

I replied I was visiting my Mama's manufacturing facility to discuss a home appliance idea. What's the idea? Tell me, Sumit said.

Well, it's actually a home appliance, a multi-purpose home appliance that I want to build.

Sumit asked, tell me in detail.

I will let you know in 10-15 days.

Sumit replied, Hmmm, well, manufacturing is a good path to consider and these days Government is promoting 'Make in India' and especially you can consider getting into Defence manufacturing.

I said that's too big to attempt at this stage. Maybe If I get through this home appliance idea successfully, then, in another 2-3 years, I can consider getting into Defence manufacturing.

Sumit also talked about his colleague who was also looking to partner with people in order to start an entrepreneurial venture. I knew many people harvest entrepreneurial ambitions, but very few take the plunge. So, I was sure that Sumit's colleague belonged in that category and therefore I did not take that seriously.

However, Sumit and I continued to talk about manufacturing for the next 10-12 days. Sumit also suggested to me to talk to one of our college mates, yea from Mechanical Engineering background as well, about the steps needed to start manufacturing a home appliance. Of course, I did call this college mate of ours and to my surprise, he did attend my call and provided me valuable contacts in order to get going in the manufacturing business.

Why was I surprised by the positive response from this college mate? Well, in my last 5-6 struggling years, I did try to talk to as well as meet many of my college buddies. And most of them have got busy in their own marital life. They hardly have any time to listen to you. Either they are busy in the office meetings or they are busy at the home meetings. I guess that's the pattern of a typical middle-class family. Get a degree, gain some work experience, go on dates, marry, and then family. No One can fault this pattern. This is a well-established pattern. Whoever falls outside of this pattern is a pariah, to put it mildly.

In the past, I had tried to talk to many of the college buddies on the prospect of going back into the corporate job. However, the response was mostly negative. People didn't even have the time to forward my CV to the HR department of their respective companies.

I had now come to terms with this harsh reality. There are no grudges against any one of them. That's the nature of the well-established pattern that I just talked about.

Even my own family members would taunt every now and then. The taunts could be extremely severe and there is no point elaborating on those taunts here.

Therefore, one begins to despise all those lovely phrases we used to hear or read in school days, 'family that eats together lives together' or 'Love is what every family needs'. I guess success is what everyone's family desires, monetary success, I mean. With success, all these lovely phrases 'family that eats together lives together' or 'Love is what every family needs' look cool. Without this success, all the lovely phrases turn into nasty phrases.

I am not grudging any one of these realities. But it's a given fact. Not even your family members will treat you well if you haven't got the case to show some sort of monetary success.

More so, in my case, having earned my engineering degree, then, working in the sunshine IT sector, then, traveling abroad for an onsite assignment, then, a master's degree, and then, finally came down crashing to good 6-7 years of absolute misery. The real estate sector had crashed and I could not make any successful inroads into that sector. Sure, I gained valuable experience in the fields of digital marketing, data analysis, in-depth knowledge of the Indian real estate sector. But all these experiences did not help me in getting a job. I applied to many companies including in India and abroad, and all I had was 'rejection'. I couldn't understand the reasons for 'rejection', but, that's all I got.

Therefore, with this reality check, I was extremely skeptical or afraid to get into the manufacturing sector. What if this one fails too? What if I get stuck in the middle of the product development? What if I end up not having the right amount of money to at least build samples of this product?

Therefore, I rejected the idea of getting into manufacturing altogether and instead focused again on finding a job, no matter if it takes time. I continued applying to companies, however, in the meantime, I also decided to build a prototype for this Mosquito problem.

Chapter 2

Building the prototype

My typical morning involved promoting my real estate platforms for about 2 hours, then, sending job applications to various companies in India and abroad, and then, finally, putting my mind and energy into developing this 'Mosquito' prototype.

During my interaction with Mama, I had already conceptualized the design of the prototype. However, the challenge was to develop this design in 3D modeling. I had no access to CAD software. I did contact some trainees on LinkedIn who were practicing 3D Modeling using popular CAD software such as ProE, SolidWorks, Catia. All those contacts proved futile as each one of them wanted some compensation, at least Rs 10000. Now, I had to think of other ways to build the prototype.

What did I do? I contacted 2-3 carpenters who could build a frame for this prototype for me from waste wood. It was a challenge in itself to first convince these carpenters to build a frame and then explain to them the dimensions of this frame. After pursuing many of such carpenters, one of them finally agreed to do it for Rs 225.

I gave him the dimensions and drew a sketch on a piece of paper. He understood the design and took out some waste wood. He then, cut the wood to the required size and then stitched or bolted together all the different parts. All it took him was mere 45-50 minutes. I said to him, not bad, Rs 225 for 45-50 minutes of work. He smiled and said, what sir, anyone else will not do this kind of work and even if someone agrees, he will charge a minimum of Rs 600. I said I will give you Rs 600 if the product becomes successful. He is still waiting though.

Once the frame was ready, the next challenge was to get the parts to fit into this wooden frame. Firstly, I started to look for different parts online including on Amazon, Flipkart, and Indiamart. There was no supplier or manufacturer who was supplying the parts as per my specifications.

What were the parts that I was searching for? A motor, blades, and UV light. These were my starting parts. Thereafter, I also wanted to do some chemistry tests in my prototype.

However, the physical parts were difficult to find. As far as Chemistry tests were concerned, I was confident of getting it right as it was 100% in my hands.

I searched for motors and could not find one. Of course, there were motors, but most were of the bigger dimensions. Finding the small UV light was a challenge as well.

I won't dwell at all on the chemistry part as I believe this is the USP of my product.

I contacted some auto parts manufacturers in Delhi NCR as well as in Gujarat. This was my first interaction with any manufacturer of a sort. And the impression I got was very bad. Most of these suppliers or manufacturers firstly want to deal with bulk buyers and secondly, they don't want to answer too many questions.

Since I was looking for something specific, most of them hung up the phone saying, 'you ask too many questions' or 'you don't want to buy at all and simply wasting our time'.

This practice continued for days. I was frustrated as neither I was able to get any call from the job applications that I was sending nor I was able to get any positive response from these manufacturers or suppliers. I said to myself, if this is how it's going to go, then, forget this Mosquito idea altogether.

However, in every tough situation, there are only 2 ways. Either you feel let down and cry or you just keep on moving. I chose the latter and kept on moving. This is not to show my bravery. I simply had no other choice but to keep on moving. Or one can say, I had nothing to lose in trying out this Mosquito idea prototype.

So, every morning, I continued with my routine. Promote the real estate platform, make job applications, and work towards the prototype for this Mosquito idea. Nothing was happening, absolutely nothing. Sometimes nothing is beautiful, well, I will not go into this 'NOTHING' concept as this is so spiritual that maybe the accomplished Gurus might take offense on my explanation of this 'NOTHING' concept.

I kept on searching and contacting manufacturers and suppliers for the AC motor that is compact yet consumes low power. I even broadened my search to China. Yes, I logged into Alibaba and started searching for parts that I wanted so badly. After a struggle of almost 3 weeks, I could find something useful. An axial fan. Yes, this was something that came close to the dimensions I was looking for. At the same time, I could find the desired UV light. Having found the parts on the Chinese platform, I started to search for traders who were dealing in such parts in India. And for the first time in my life, I came face to face with the power and influence of Chinese manufacturing. It is humongous, believe me. Indian manufacturing pales in comparison to Chinese manufacturing. No wonder, India has a trade deficit of 60+ billion US dollars (4.2 Lacs Crores Rupees) with China. I guess, not just India, most countries in the world have massive trade deficits with China. However, I was least bothered about all these fancy concepts such as trade deficits. It's not in my hands. It's in fact, not in any of the entrepreneurs' hands.

I was able to find the traders that were dealing in the parts that I wanted badly. I contacted 3 of them. Again, despite being an ordinary trader, all these traders were so unprofessional or even rude in dealing with a small buyer like me. These traders don't treat single item buyers well. They respond as if they are doing a favor to a small buyer like me. However, I agreed to buy the desired parts at whatever price they quoted. I did not even bargain. I knew, if I started bargaining, they will simply hang up the phone. So, one of the traders gave the address and contact details of the warehouse in Noida, where I can get the desired axial fan. It costed me around Rs 900 per piece. Of course, I wanted only one to build my prototype.

UV lights were equally difficult to find. I mean, the UV lights of specific configuration that I wanted. However, having come in contact with the Chinese goods traders, I knew it was only a matter of time before I found the desired UV lights. And I did indeed find the traders. That was some success. After spending almost a month to find the desired parts, I now started to look for Chemistry tests. That part was relatively easier for me as I had full control over that aspect.

I finally got the desired parts, however, there was a problem. Even though the parts were close to the specifications that I wanted, they did not fit in the wooden frame that I had developed. So, I again reached out to that Carpenter and asked him to make another frame with slightly different dimensions. He said, come tomorrow and I will do it. I had no other option but to visit him the next day. Even though, I realized coming back the next day will cost me Rs 60-70 more. Waste of money.

I visited the carpenter the next day, and he took almost an hour to finish the wooden frame as per the new dimensions. This time though, he charged Rs 350. No less. No bargaining. So, while on my way home, I was a little peeved at the extra money that I had to spend on this wooden frame. Why was I in a hurry to build this wooden frame first? I kept asking myself. Well, that's how entrepreneurship goes, it's so difficult to get all the steps correct.

On a positive note, now, I had all the desired parts, frames, screws, results from chemical tests. It was 5 PM in the evening when I reached home. I did nothing but started assembling everything together. It took me almost 3 hours to assemble everything. And Finally, on 1st May 2018, I had the prototype ready for my Mosquito idea. Bravo! I was delighted. I had dinner and went for a walk and as soon as I came back, I switched on the appliance. It was great to see it worked exactly the way I had envisioned. Now, I kept on checking how many mosquitoes it caught. 40-45 minutes into the running of this appliance, I could see 5-6 mosquitoes. Wow, I slept afterward keeping the appliance switched on. Wow, next morning I could see massive numbers of mosquitoes in the appliance. I was delighted. The prototype became the ultimate solution for our home. We did not use any other mosquito solution thereafter.

So much so, that I started to use this Mosquito prototype in different rooms. 30 minutes in one closed room, catch all the mosquitoes there, 30 minutes in another closed room, and catch the mosquitoes in that room as well. And finally, keep the appliance switched on for the whole night either in one of the rooms or in the living room. However, I made sure all the windows and doors of the apartment were closed.

Next night, I kept the windows open. What it meant was, a new stream of mosquitoes will continue to enter the apartment. This new stream of mosquitoes was caught, however, some mosquitoes continued to fly around. As per my design, the appliance was meant to simulate the human body for mosquitoes. This meant, if there are humans in the room along with the Mosquiter Product (another human for mosquitoes), then, some of the mosquitoes will hover around humans and some will hover around Mosquiter product. That's how the product had been conceived. Therefore, it was not surprising to see some mosquitoes hover around the room despite Mosquiter product being switched on.

In other words, I realized, for best use, the Mosquiter product shall be used in a closed empty room to catch all the mosquitoes. Once all the mosquitoes were caught, I could sleep peacefully with Mosquiter product still switched on. However, doors, as well as windows, were closed.

I tested the prototype and results were incredible. We simply did not use any other mosquito solutions such as coils, net, repellents, refills, etc in our home. My family members were impressed with the results as well. Within a week, the appliance was replete with dead mosquitoes. I did not throw those dead mosquitoes in order to show to people the startling results of my efforts.

I was excited as a 3-year-old kid. I was beaming with energy. I discussed the Mosquiter prototype with a couple of my friends. Of course, one being Sumit and the other being Sunil. Sumit was truly glad and in fact, went on to the extent of calling me next millionaire (USD terms). He promised to visit my apartment in the coming 2-3 days to see the prototype and its results.

Sunil, who had moved to the UK along with his family was equally ecstatic. Sunil had seen my struggling 6-7 years from close quarters. He, in fact, partnered with me in the development of an online real estate platform. He is not only a gifted coder but also a compassionate human being. I met him Via the SEO (Search Engine Optimization). After my return from Switzerland, I was looking for software development companies in Faridabad to develop my real estate platform. I contacted many people in my network as well as on LinkedIn. However, nothing worked. And now, I started to search for software development companies in Faridabad. And Sunil's website came on top of organic results. I had zero ideas about SEO at that time and how SEO worked. However, that was not my concern. My main concern was getting on board the right software development company for the development of the real estate platform. I contacted 3 companies that showed up on the first page on that day.

2 of them looked highly unprofessional on the phone itself. I rejected them then and there. Sunil responded positively and we fixed up the meeting the next day. His office (home) was in Sector 21, whereas I lived in sector 28. It was just a distance of 3-4 kilometers. I drove down to Sunil's home, and we had a detailed chat and he clearly understood my requirements and he agreed to develop the real estate platform in MVC.net. That was the latest technology at that time. I said, cool, let's start the work soon. Initially, he agreed to do the project for a fixed amount. However, during the course of our interaction, he came on board and ended up becoming one of the partners in the whole online real estate platform business. That business did not flourish is another story, however, we continued to remain friends and discussed literally

everything in India from politics to bureaucracy, to roads, to infrastructure, to the economy, etc. The conversations were always engaging.

Sunil, then, left to the UK and we still continued to talk on FB, WhatsApp, as well as on phone about various ideas. I did discuss 2-3 more ideas with him including an idea on the car-sharing App. However, we had been in online (So-called 'Tech') domain for so long, we had come to the terms that developing an App is one thing but getting people to accept that App is another beast altogether and that requires a huge amount of resources.

Therefore, most of the online (Tech) ideas were not enthusing us anymore. I called up Sunil on WhatsApp:

Hey Sunil, I had an idea

Sunil said, yea, tell me about it.

I said it's about mosquitoes.

Sunil, what? I was expecting another online (Tech) idea.

I said, no no, Online ideas are passe. I have this mosquito idea that falls under the manufacturing domain.

Sunil said, sounds impressive, so tell me about this mosquito idea.

Well, Sunil, as you know, I moved to Noida in October 2017, and in March 2018 (spring season) I was literally pissed off with a deluge of mosquitoes in our home in Noida. The problem was so big that I decided to build a prototype for our home. It took me almost 6 weeks to build this prototype and results are astounding.

Sunil replied, brilliant Sachin. I think this is it. This will work. If you have caught so many mosquitoes with your appliance and if you are so delighted, then, this can work. Mosquitoes are a pan-India problem, and if you have been able to solve it, then, it can be magical.

I said, yea, it can be made on a large scale. However, I have very little idea about manufacturing. Moreover, I have zero money at this stage to even think about attempting this idea.

Sunil said, let's discuss this again tomorrow, I am going to a meeting now. And surely, we can find a way out.

I said, alright, let's talk again tomorrow about manufacturing possibilities for this idea.

The next day, Sunil called me again. It was around 7:30 PM in India. And of course, it was the post-lunch session in the UK. Sunil had 20-30 minutes to talk about this idea. Sunil again started to inquire about the technicalities of this Mosquiter prototype. I explained to him that this prototype works on the principles of attraction & suction. The Mosquiter Prototype basically simulates the human body to attract mosquitoes and then suck them up by the use of low power high airflow fan. Sunil was truly impressed by the idea as well as the prototype that I had developed.

Chapter 3

Understanding supply chain and Estimating the amount of money required to get into manufacturing

Now, we started to talk about possible ways of manufacturing this Mosquiter product on a larger scale. Of course, the conversation boiled down to the resources. With resources, I mean money. I had no money and therefore it was tricky to think about ways to aggregate resources to build this Mosquiter product on a larger scale. Sunil suggested, he could loan me some amount (3-4 Lacs Rupees). However, building about 1000 such appliances would require more money than Rupees 3-4 Lacs. My point was that I can start by building 1000 appliances first and then sell these 1000 pieces and gauge customers' feedback.

I knew from my own unsuccessful entrepreneurial experience that if I could sell 1000s of such appliances to customers across India, then, getting venture funding from investors might be possible in order to scale the whole set-up.

With this thought in mind, I said to Sunil, let me first calculate the cost per piece for Mosquiter product. We discontinued our conversation. I again focused on sourcing the right suppliers to develop this Mosquiter product for the first 1000 customers.

I started to talk to some suppliers or manufacturers from India. Most of these suppliers were mainly from Delhi NCR or Gujarat. Basically, I was looking to source just 2 parts.

Fan with specific blade angle and LED Light. I had specifications in my mind. I also contacted the traders that I had contacted during the prototype building stage. But those traders were supplying the parts at high prices. I did not care about the cost during the prototype building stage, however, now cost was the key. The cost will determine the selling price. And the selling price will determine the acceptability of the product. I had determined that the final selling price shall not be more than Rupees 1000. So, I was OK with the selling price of Rupees 800 or 900.

Therefore, with this selling price range in my mind, I started to do the reverse calculations. With reverse calculations, I deduced the price of buying Fan and LED Light. With this price in mind, I started to contact many suppliers including in India and in China.

My next month went into this. Sometimes, I would get the parts with desired specifications, but the price will be high. Sometimes, I will get the right price, but then, specifications will be inferior. This one month was truly frustrating. Having talked to many suppliers in India, I came to the conclusion that it's a waste of time and energy talking to them. I will elaborate later as to why talking to Indian manufacturers was a waste of time and energy. Now, I focused solely on Chinese suppliers. My conversations with Chinese suppliers took place mainly on the Alibaba portal. I contacted approximately 200 such suppliers in China. They would send me the quote. I would ask them some technical questions and they would happily respond to my queries. This whole process continued for many days. I started to filter down the right suppliers and now the conversations with these filtered suppliers moved to WeChat. I installed the WeChat app on my laptop. Yes, I still do not own a smartphone. I started to use Bluestacks simulator to install apps on my laptop. And thus, WeChat became my most used App during that month.

I got quotes from 6 filtered suppliers with regards to the Fan. These 6 suppliers agreed to offer me the Fan with a specific blade angle. However, to do so, they would have to develop a new mold. And they were willing to do that. Well, this is one of the major differences between a Chinese seller and an Indian seller. An Indian seller would snub me as soon as I started to discuss specific requirements. They would simply say 'Lena ho to lo, varna time waste mat Karo'. Whereas a Chinese supplier will listen to my requirements knowing fully well that I am going to buy just 1000 pieces. However, they would listen and reply within a day.

The 6 suppliers who agreed to offer me the Fan with a specific blade angle gave me the near-identical price. Barring a minor difference in specifications such as noise level, airflow volume, the Fan was almost identical. However, I had an issue with this Fan. Its thickness was more than what I had planned. This high thickness or depth would mean that my final Mosquiter product will look 5-6 inches thick or its depth would be 5-6 inches.

Therefore, I again started to contact other suppliers. Days passed by and my search for a perfect solution was not yielding anything. Somehow, I was able to make contacts with another 3 suppliers who were making sleek Fan. These 3 suppliers also agreed to offer me the Fan with a specific blade angle. However, the price of this sleek Fan was almost 2 times that of the Fan offered by the previous 6 suppliers. This was a big conundrum for me. Whether to accept the high price or slightly higher thickness of the Fan.

I went back to my Prototype. It was already 4 inches thick. I thought about the 5 inches thick final product for another 2-3 days. I visualized it. I said to myself, maybe the design of the final product can be developed in such a way that 5 inches thickness or depth doesn't look too big. I started to look for some 5-6 inches thick home decoration products on Google. I could find some alloy wheels, mirrors, and even wall clocks. With these ideas in mind, I started to visualize my own final product in a better way. I had already thought of developing the Mosquiter product along the lines of a wall clock. Therefore, finding some 5-6 inches thick wall clock designs further enhanced my confidence in opting for a slightly thicker Fan.

Now, I again contacted the previous 6 suppliers who had agreed to offer me the Fan with a specific blade angle. This time though, I negotiated with them for a better price. However, with just 1000 pieces of buying power, I had little room for a reduction in price. I finally settled on the supplier with the best terms and prices. I asked the supplier to deliver me the sample Fan first. The supplier agreed to send me the sample free of cost, but I had to pay for the courier charges. I agreed to that. I provided them my address and asked for their bank info which they duly provided.

I added their bank account to my online banking platform. I made the payment and they shipped the sample Fan to me. I guess, within 10 days, the sample Fan was delivered to me. It took 10 days because the supplier had to make a specific blade angle using the 3D printing technique.

The Fan looked superb. The Fan worked as per the mentioned specifications. I was happy with the sample Fan and therefore my confidence in the Fan supplier grew.

Now, I still had to source the LED Light. I was again looking for LED Light with unique specifications for my Mosquiter product. It was very very tough.

Since the Fan with a specific blade angle was 8 inches in Diameter, therefore, I had to look for the LED Light with Diameter not exceeding 6 inches. The diameter of LED Light could be less than 6 inches but certainly not more than 6 inches. Here again, I faced difficulties in finding the suppliers. One supplier from Gujarat was offering 6 inches LED Light, however, the wattage of that LED Light was too low. Despite that, I asked them to send me the sample. The supplier from Gujarat agreed to send me the sample but the sample was not free of cost. I had to transfer the sample LED Light fee along with the courier fee before they dispatched the sample to me.

The sample arrived 3 days later. It was as per the specifications mentioned. And therefore, as stated on the product, the wattage of that LED Light was too low. I started to look for other suppliers in India. Most of them were offering the same product. Either I increase the Diameter or settle for low wattage. I could not increase the Diameter of LED light nor could I settle for low wattage.

Therefore, my focus again shifted to China. I logged onto the Alibaba portal again. This time though, I was primarily searching for LED Light. I contacted about 12 suppliers. One thing I noticed about LED Light was that both Indian and Chinese suppliers were offering standard products. The 6-inch diameter LED Light will always come with low wattage.

I started to talk to those 12 LED Light suppliers. From the very beginning, I would tell them that I need 6 inches or less Diameter LED Light with higher wattage. Two of those twelve suppliers agreed to take my specific requirements to their technical team. They responded to me positively.

However, they put down a condition on me. The condition was that I shall order a minimum of 5000 pieces. I asked them, why do I need to order 5000 pieces? They explained to me that in order for them to deliver LED Lights with my unique specifications, they will have to open new mold and that would cost me money. If I go for only 1000 pieces, then, the price per piece will increase because the cost of opening a new mold will be distributed for just 1000 pieces. However, If I order 5000 pieces, then, the cost of opening a new mold will substantially go down. I could understand their reasoning. However, there was no way, I could order for 5000 pieces. I wanted the 1000

LED Lights with my unique specifications. I again asked one of those 2 suppliers to talk to the technical team.

After about a week, the one and only supplier agreed to deliver me 1000 LED Lights with my unique specifications at a slightly higher price. About 5% more than the actual price of a standard LED Light. I agreed to that 5% increase in price. I knew, no one else would deliver me 1000 pieces of 6 inches diameter LED Lights with my own unique specifications. Therefore, it was a good deal. LED Lights discussions and negotiations took more time than that of a Fan. However, it was worth it. Deep down I knew, If this Mosquiter product is accepted well in the market, then, I had already developed my supply chain. I would source 2 parts - Fan and LED Light - from China and the rest of the parts from India.

The rest of the parts included wiring, socket, screws, pipes, chemical solutions to simulate a human body, packaging, printing, stickers, and microtubes. Sourcing these parts was relatively straight forward. I would contact basically 4-5 suppliers in India and finalize one among them.

Other than the sourcing of parts, I had to manufacture the Frame or the body of the appliance here in India. At this stage, I was merely concerned with finding the raw material cost as well as the cost of building such a frame in India. I contacted one of my college friends 'Bansal' who was in a plastic manufacturing set-up.

Bansal responded to me saying we can meet at the coming weekend. I visited his set-up in Nangloi. Nangloi is an undeveloped industrial zone in western Delhi. I took Metro rail from Noida to reach his workplace. He asked one of his staff members to pick me up from Metro station. The staff member came on a motorbike along with a spare helmet. I wore the helmet and sat on the rear seat of the bike. I was visiting Nangloi for the very first time. The area was really undeveloped. Basically, it's still a village that has got some connectivity from the main city. However, the roads, drainage, as well as houses were all semi-developed. It took us some 15 minutes from Metro station to reach his workplace.

I reached there and waited for Bansal to come. He came 10 minutes later. He offered me a bottle of water and started to explain to me his business. Bansal had been in that business for almost 12 years. Therefore, he had a deep understanding of the manufacturing business. He knew what is a mold, he knew the various mold makers in the city, he knew the raw material requirements, basically, he knew everything that I wanted to know.

We had a detailed discussion. I explained my product details to him. He asked me how would my final product look like? I said it would very much be similar to a wall clock. I showed some existing wall clock design on Google images. He could visualize the wall clock. He said to me, you would need 2 molds - one for the front cover and one for the back cover. He also said to me that the total weight of raw material required to build front as well as the back cover would be around 700-800 grams. And if you are going to develop your appliance in ABS, then, 700-800 grams of material would cost you around Rupees 120. On top of this raw material cost, mold set-up cost would be around Rs 30 for both the covers. Therefore, approximately, it would cost me Rupees 150 per piece to develop the frames for Mosquiter product. That cost looked extremely high to me. If I add costs of other parts, then, the total cost per piece would exceed Rs 500. I came home with the thought, that, it's foolish to build such a product. My point was that the cost is exceeding my set target. If it costs me more than Rs 500 per piece to develop the Mosquiter product, then, surely, I won't be able to sell the final product for less than Rupees 1200. Other than the manufacturing cost, I have to add marketing cost, replacement cost, margin, taxes, costs charged by online platforms. Therefore, I was so dejected knowing that the cost would exceed Rs 500 per piece.

It took me 2 days to come to terms with it. I knew I can not redesign the product in order to bring down the cost. It was not at all possible. Because if I tried to bring the cost down, the final product will be functionally inferior.

I called Sumit to discuss the selling price for a Mosquiter product.
I said, Sumit, the cost of developing this Mosquiter product is going upward of Rupees 500. That would mean selling price in excess of Rupees 1200. Do you think people would be able to buy such an appliance for Rs 1200 or Rs 1300?
Sumit said it would have been ideal if the product was sold for less than Rupees 1000.
I said, it's not happening because I can not compromise on the quality.

Sumit had no answer and responded by saying, let's keep thinking for 2-3 days and maybe there is a solution to it.

I said, OK, and we hung up the phone to talk at a later stage.

However, I was restless. I wanted some reassurance right then. I called up Sunil. Since Sunil was in the UK, he would reject my call and call me back from his computer or some other apparatus. That would mean we could talk for a longer duration virtually for free.

Sunil called me back, yea, Sachin, you were saying something.

I said, yea, the point is that the cost of developing this Mosquiter product is exceeding Rs 500 which would mean a selling price of Rs 1200 or 1300.

Sunil responded by saying, don't worry, if the product is functionally effective, then, India is a large enough country and there are segments of people who would be willing to spend even Rs 2000. Therefore, you should just focus on developing the best possible product that is effective as well as aesthetic.

Sunil's words really reassured me. We continued to talk for another 5-6 minutes and then hung up the phone. I was feeling a little confident now.

However, I was still adamant to keep the cost per piece to be as low as possible. With this thought in mind, I started to visualize a typical customer for my product. I knew the selling price of this Mosquiter product is going to be in excess of Rs 1300. Therefore, my whole focus now shifted to the customer segment who would be willing to pay this price.

I had done business management and I took out those fancy theorems or frameworks that were taught to us during the master's program. One of the simple yet effective frameworks was about defining 'Product', 'Customer', 'Region', 'Channel'.

I had already visualized and worked out my product in great detail. Now, it was time to think about the customer. I knew the Mosquitoes' problem was a pan-India problem. All segments of society, be it adults, senior citizens, kids, high income or low-income groups, everyone was pained by the mosquitoes across all of India except maybe mountainous regions. Therefore, I wasn't bothered about finding the market size. I knew it was large enough to serve and grow.

However, at the same time, I knew my limitations. I knew that I had little resources (money) to spend on marketing campaigns. In the beginning, I can only reach out to people by using online channels. Therefore, I started to segment my customer by the 'channel' that I can utilize to reach out to that particular customer segment. And in my case, since I could only utilize the 'online channel', therefore, I started to visualize who my ideal customer is going to be.

I started using Google Data including Google trend, Keyword search volume. I took 2-3 days to collect and analyze that data. Based on that data, I realized my ideal customer would be someone who is living in a new upcoming housing society and he/she is employed with a disposable income of around Rs 50000 +. With that ideal customer in mind, I started to now ask myself, how many of such people will exist in India? Well, Google's keyword search volume gave a little inkling. However, I had no other means to arrive at the exact number for such people. I said to myself, if Google keyword search volume is accurate, then, I don't need to worry about the total number of customers that I can serve. That number itself was large enough to target in the beginning. And even if, 1% of such people buy and appreciate my product, then, there it is. I have hit the jackpot. I guess this was a typical entrepreneurial calculation. But that entrepreneurial calculation was based on some data.

Therefore, in order to define my customer, I was able to define the 'channel' to reach out to that defined customer. In other words, my limited resources dictated my ideal customer. Now, 'Product' is defined, 'Customer' is defined, 'Channel' is defined, what about the 'Region'? Again, my 'Channel' dictated my definition of 'Region' as well. With the online 'Channel', I could reach out to practically every 'Region' that is suffering from Mosquito problem. So, my 'Region' was practically all of India that can be reached by online 'Channel'. I knew, if the product is highly effective, then, other customer segments could open out as well. However, in order to stick to my Management Framework, I had now arrived at a detailed analysis of the 'Product', 'Customer', 'Channel', and 'Region'. It may appear simplistic, but that's how I was visualizing my whole strategy. My focus though was primarily on developing an effective and aesthetic product. Deep down, I knew, with an effective functional product, I would find something in the Indian market. 'Product' has to be wow. That's it. That was my strategy. Focus on Product, Product, and Product.

By this time, I had built a successful prototype. I had developed the supply chain to source different parts from China as well as from India to manufacture 1000 pieces. I had also written down the whole strategy including the 'Product', 'Customer', 'Channel', and 'Region'. Everything was in place. Yea, from the outside, everything looked in place. Can I take this whole exercise that I had accomplished to an angel investor or a venture capital firm, I asked myself? The answer was 'No'. From my unsuccessful startup experience, I knew all these investors would turn me down because of 3 reasons:

One, all these investors even though smart still end up following a herd mentality. If the trend is to invest in the consumer tech business, then, everyone would chase consumer tech startups. If the trend is to invest in social platforms, then, everyone would chase social platforms.

Secondly, all these investors had the propensity to invest primarily in the Tech domain. I hadn't heard anyone calling a new manufacturing business a 'startup'.

Thirdly, all these investors primarily invested in startups that have some customers to show for.

Therefore, with this in the background, I decided not to waste my energy in chasing angel investors or venture firms. So, how do I raise money to manufacture 1000 pieces, I kept asking myself? I knew I could rely on Sunil for some 3-4 Lacs Rupees. However, I also knew that I needed approximately Rs 8 lacs to even start thinking about manufacturing 1000 pieces. The amount needed could certainly exceed Rs 8 Lacs, but it won't be less than that. Days passed by and I had no answers as to how would I accumulate the required capital. At the same time, I still kept applying to job openings, I still kept working on my real estate platform. However, from all sides, there was no positive response. 'Nothing was happening', literally, nothing.

It was already the first week of June, and I had told to myself that by the first week of July I should set the ball in motion come what may. I had given myself one month to either accumulate the required money or to abandon the idea. Now, I also started to discuss this idea with my other family members. Knowing my past failures, they told me to forget this idea. Their line of thinking was, it's a lot of work and without money, you can't do anything. Moreover, they were also of the view that such products might not be accepted in the market. They instead asked me to accumulate Rs 3-4 Lacs and then travel to Germany on a job seeking Visa to search for a good job there. I gave it a thought. I knew, starting up would not only require money but at the same time would also require plenty of time. It would also mean a high probability of failure. On the other hand, accumulating Rs 3-4 Lacs and traveling to Germany on a job seeking Visa for 3-4 months might bring me a decent job.

I thought for a couple of days and realized that these days job applications are mostly sent online. And the first couple of interviews are mostly conducted on phone or Skype. Therefore, it does not matter, if I live in India or Germany, I can still send job applications to companies in Germany. Why only Germany? Because before this Mosquiter idea gripped my mind in March, I was sending job applications to German companies and 3 of those companies interviewed me on phone and one among them in fact, invited me to Germany for the final round of interviews. Therefore, there was a strong case to be made for visiting Germany on job seeking Visa.

Days were passing by and I was not able to arrange the required capital to manufacture 1000 Mosquiter pieces. I was also seriously contemplating going to Germany on a job seeking Visa. I called Sunil and shared my dichotomy with him. He already knew about the Mosquiter product. He was aware of each & every stage of my work on developing the Mosquiter product. He also knew about my travel to Germany for the final round of interviews. Knowing all the facts, he also suggested to me that traveling to Germany on a job seeking Visa would be a waste of time and money. Because 'truth be told', most of the applications these days are sent online and the first round of interviews are mostly conducted on phone or Skype. Therefore, he suggested to me to keep working on Mosquiter idea as well as keep applying to jobs in Germany.

I knew by being physically present in Germany, I might improve my chances of getting a job by 5-10%. However, spending borrowed money on lodging, traveling, and sitting in a room all day, and sending online job applications in Germany didn't appeal to me. I can rather do that exercise from India by incurring no cost at all. And I had been doing that exercise for practically 1 year now. Therefore, I had made up my mind that I am not at all traveling to Germany on a job seeking Visa. I stayed committed to sending online job applications to Germany from India and kept working on my Mosquiter product.

Why wasn't I applying to Indian companies? I did that, and after thousands of rejections, I had realized that I ain't going to get a job in India because of 3 reasons.

Firstly, the supply of talent is huge in India and any company hiring me would instead hire someone who is working in a similar role in another company.

Secondly, I had worked as well as completed my master's in a German-speaking region in Europe and my university was counted as the top university in the German-speaking region. Therefore, they would appreciate my experiences and education slightly better than any other Indian employer.

Thirdly, employers in India have double standards when it comes to failed entrepreneurship. They all would speak positively in media on the need for encouraging entrepreneurship as well as risk-taking. However, when it came to hiring potential employees, they all would play it safe and instead hire or poach someone who is working in a similar role in another company. I guess it makes business sense as well.

Therefore, I had stopped applying to Indian companies. All my energies were focused on sending job applications to German companies. I stuck to my routine and religiously followed it. It was already the end of June 2018 and I had no positive news. I still hadn't arranged the required capital to manufacture 1000 pieces for Mosquiter product. Frustration would be a mild word, I was really intense, super intense and charged up to crack the code. Either get a job or set the ball in motion to manufacture 1000 pieces of this Mosquiter product. The intensity was so high that I couldn't sleep for some nights. I wasn't worried, I was simply intense and kept on thinking.

Now, I called my Mama again. This time to tell him that I am going ahead with the development of Mosquiter product. I did not waste any time discussing the merits or demerits of going ahead with this plan. I simply asked him if he could assist me with Rupees 4 Lacs. He was speechless. He did not say anything for a few seconds and then hung up the phone saying he would talk to me next week.

That next week did not come. It was already the first week of July. However, Raju called me. Raju is a property consultant and I had known him for almost 3 years now. We would share property leads with each other. Basically, he would provide me Noida, Gurgaon leads and I would provide him Delhi leads. The real estate market was so low that we hadn't completed any transaction so far on leads given to each other.

This time though, he called me to work on a commercial real estate transaction. He asked me to show some industrial plots in Noida to a potential renter. I said to myself, maybe this time, Raju and I get lucky and crack this commercial real estate transaction. Raju forwarded my number to the potential renter and also provided me the phone number of that renter. I called up that renter and fixed-up time and a meeting place in Noida. I had some very good options to show him.

The next day, the renter and I met at the pre-decided place at 11 AM. I took him for site visits to industrial plots in sector 81, sector 83, and NSEZ. In about 5 hours, we visited 5 very good industrial plots. The renter seemed to like 2 options out of those 5 visited sites. The monthly rental for those 2 plots was approximately 1.5 Lacs Rupees. Basically, the renter wanted a plot of around 8000 to 10000 square feet. And at Rs 20 per square feet, the rent would come down to about Rs. 1.5 Lacs. If the deal goes through, then, the landlord will initiate the work on the plot including flooring, sheds, and arranging for water & electricity supply.

I was thinking, if the deal goes through, then we will get a 1-month rental in commissions from both the renter as well as the plot owner. I will keep the commission from the plot owner and Raju will keep the commission from the renter. The prospect of Rs 1.5 Lacs looked lucrative to me. And the renter wanted to close the transaction soon. However, 4-5 days had passed by and I did not get any feedback either from Raju or the renter. At the same time, the plot owner was constantly calling me to inquire about the status of the deal. I followed up with Raju as well as with the renter, and there was no positive news. I was dejected. My hope of accumulating capital for the Mosquiter product evaporated again. I discussed this again with Sunil and he was equally helpless as well. He told me that he would talk to some people in the UK about my idea and prototype and get back to me in a couple of days.

Sunil did call me 2 days later and he provided me one contact number. It was of Himanshu. Himanshu was basically working in the UK for several years and he had some contacts in venture capital firms. He himself had invested a small amount in some startups as well. Himanshu was in Gurgaon at that time.

The next day, I called Himanshu and I explained my product and plan to him. He was impressed with the idea as well as the prototype that I had developed. He said to me, getting venture funding for manufacturing set-up would be difficult. He instead asked me what if I could give a demo of my prototype to some other companies who were working in Mosquito repellent field. He asked me to write an email to the Senior Manager of the Mosquito repellent division of Godrej Group as well as Mortein.

The next day, I sent the following email to the Senior Manager of the Mosquito repellent division of Godrej Group.

"*Dear Madam,*
I just had a word with Himanshu Nautiyal and he asked me to write to you.
It was so kind of Himanshu Nautiyal to introduce me to you and your team.

This year in February, I moved to Noida. However, in March, I faced an unexpected deluge of mosquitoes. I tried everything at my home, from Hit to All Out to Local mosquito sticks, but the problem persisted.

Frustrated with this deluge of mosquitoes, I started to make a prototype to solve this problem. 2 months down the line, I had developed a prototype and now I have been using this prototype in my home for some time and I am delighted with the results. Since I started using this prototype, I have not used any other mosquito repellent or solution in my home. The prototype works superbly.

Now, I have set the ball in motion to manufacture this product and take this to market. As suggested by Himanshu, I would be pleased to discuss this with you in order to find out the synergies between us.

Thanks and look to hear from you".

And I also sent another email to Mortein.

"Dear Madam,

I just had a word with Himanshu Nautiyal and he asked me to write to you.

It was so kind of Himanshu Nautiyal to introduce me to you and your team.

This year in February, I moved to Noida. However, in March, I faced an unexpected deluge of mosquitoes. I tried everything at my home, from Good Knight to Fast card to Local mosquito sticks, but the problem persisted.

Frustrated with this deluge of mosquitoes, I started to make a prototype to solve this problem. 2 months down the line, I had developed a prototype and now I have been using this prototype in my home for some time and I am delighted with the results. Since I started using this prototype, I have not used any other mosquito repellent or solution in my home. The prototype works superbly.

Now, I have set the ball in motion to manufacture this product and take this to market. As suggested by Himanshu, I would be pleased to discuss this with you in order to find out the synergies between us.

Thanks and look to hear from you."

Basically, For Godrej Email, I highlighted the ineffectiveness of Moretien products. Whereas for Mortein email, I highlighted the ineffectiveness of Godrej products.

And surprise surprise, I got the revert from Godrej Group Senior Manager on Thursday.

" Hi, Sachin,

Glad to know about your research and product. Do give me time to figure out who is the right person I should route you to. I shall get back to you by Wednesday next week. Thanks"

The Senior Manager promised me to revert by Wednesday next week. It was almost 5-6 days later. And I did not want to just depend on one conversation. I kept on talking to others in my network. This time, I called up Vijay. Vijay is my ex-colleague. We had worked together in an IT company. He knew me very well and we basically operated on the same energy level. We partied together and participated in fashion shows in the past. And all those were wonderful moments. Vijay also knew about my current real estate platform. I called Vijay on Thursday.

Vijay, what's up buddy? I said

Vijay, all well, just extremely occupied these days in a start-up that I co-founded with my Management school buddies.

I said, wow, what's it about?

Vijay, it's about automating manufacturing companies including warehouses.

I said, interesting, very interesting. I am also thinking of entering into the manufacturing space. Not thinking, but have actually started for the last 3 months.

Vijay, super, what's it about?

I said it's about Mosquitoes.

Vijay, what happened to the mosquitoes?

I replied, no no, nothing happened to the mosquitoes, but I have developed a prototype to catch and kill mosquitoes. It's a chemical-free, eco-friendly electric appliance.

Vijay, impressive, and how's the prototype working?

I said, superb, since the development of this prototype, I haven't used any other mosquito solution in my home.

Vijay, incredible Bhai. So, what next?

I said, thinking of manufacturing 1000 such pieces to see how the product does in the marketplace.

Vijay, yea, but manufacturing these 1000 pieces would take time and cost you money. How would you arrange this?

I replied that's why I called you Bhai. I have arranged for some amount. However, I still need about 4-5 Lacs Rupees to start manufacturing.

Vijay, Hmmm, you know, I have just entered into this start-up and cash flow is extremely tight. But give me a day or two to see what best can I do.

I said, alright, I would look to hear from you. And if you get time, then, do let me know, I can show you the prototype as well.

Vijay, cool, give me a day or two. I will call you surely.

We hung up the phone after this rather long discussion.

Vijay, however, got busy and did not reply to me for another 1 week. Meanwhile, the Senior Manager of the Godrej Group had replied to me with the following email.

" *Hi, Sachin,*

Marking Ms. Pooja Verma from our Innovation team on this mail. You may take it forward with her.

Rgds."

I did contact Pooja and she replied to me saying she would call me the next morning to discuss the whole idea and the results of the prototype.

The next morning Pooja called me up at sharp 11 AM. I went outside of my apartment because the telecom signals these days inside the apartments are rather weak. And it's a Pan India problem. I hope the government pulls up these telecom companies. Anyways, Pooja introduced herself to me. And then, I introduced myself. After the brief rounds of introduction, I started to explain to her my prototype and how it attracts and kills mosquitoes. She had already heard about suction traps. However, she could understand the difference between my prototype and other appliances available in the market. However, as per the Godrej Group policy, they were only considering investing in or supporting pollen-based ideas. I understood their line of thinking. It's extremely hard for a large conglomerate to shift its focus from current operations. Investing in or supporting new ideas outside of their pollen-based domain can be a herculean task for them. And she made it amply clear to me. We hung up the phone thanking each other for the valuable time.

After my discussion with Pooja, I sent a thank you email to the Senior Manager. I also wrote to Himanshu about what transpired between me and Pooja. Himanshu also understood Godrej Group's line of thinking. Himanshu then suggested me some online platforms to sell my first 1000 pieces. I thanked him for his efforts. However, at that stage, I was simply focused on first manufacturing 1000 pieces and therefore was looking for some sort of investment.

The next day, Vijay called me and he said, I am coming to your home in the evening. I said, cool, it would be super good to meet you. Vijay arrived at around 7:30 PM. It took him time to locate my society location despite the Google Map. Anyways, he came and we were happy to meet each other after many months. He did not come inside the apartment because he was in a hurry. However, I did show him my prototype and he was amazed. He was excited by my energy to first think of resolving Mosquitoes' problem and then developing this prototype. We started to talk about the ways in which this product could be sold in India. I told him that at present I am just focused on the online channels to sell this product. Later on, based on the market feedback, I could consider other channels. After this elaborate discussion, Vijay himself said to me that he would be able to arrange some funds. And I asked him, how much? He said, can't say now but you must get going to estimate the total investment required to manufacture 1000 pieces. I was cool with this line of thinking. We had Tea at a local tea shop and then went to our homes.

Now, my next task was to estimate the total investment required to manufacture the first 1000 pieces. I had already got a quote from Chinese suppliers. My next task was to get the final quotes from Indian suppliers for other parts including the body or frame, wiring, socket, packaging, coating solutions, netting, screws, and other supporting parts.

From the very next day onward, I started contacting suppliers for the above-mentioned parts. Indiamart platform came in handy for this exercise. For each and every part, I would basically contact 5-6 suppliers and get the best possible quote including the quality of the material. I started to make a list and based on the quote as well as on the professionalism of the salesman of those suppliers, I would put them on top of my list. I will elaborate on the professionalism aspect in great detail in the later chapters of this book.

Now, I had a fair bit of idea or a close estimate of the costs of various parts needed to manufacture 1000 pieces. However, one thing was missing. Estimating the investment required to build molds for the body or the frame for this Mosquiter product. The cost of developing the molds would classify under fixed costs. Just like one would invest in land for setting up a manufacturing plant or buying machinery. In other words, molds would come under the category of Capex. I already knew the raw material cost required to build 1000 pieces. However, I needed the molds to develop the body or frame. And I had no idea about molds.

I again contacted my manufacturing friend 'Bansal'. Last time, when I visited him, I basically got the estimate for raw material. However, this time, I was solely focused on getting the estimate for developing the molds to build the body of the product. Bansal asked me to visit him the day after tomorrow. I took 'Metro' to visit Nangloi and once again one of his staff members picked me up from the Nangloi Metro station. It was already 1:30 PM. Time for lunch.

Bansal ordered lunch and one of his staff members bought the Lunch for two of us including a tetra pack of juice. We washed our hands and started to eat our lunch. During this time, we also shared light-hearted banter from our college days. We talked about various characters from our class of Mechanical Engineering including Sumit. Bansal was also stunned to know that Sumit had changed completely from college days. As we were enjoying our Lunch, Bhanu called me. Bhanu is also one of our buddies. Bhanu and I continue to meet regularly. However, this time, I gave the phone to Bansal and they had a good conversation about college days. I told Bansal that Bhanu knows about my new product and he is always suggesting me to develop an aesthetic product. Well, lunch was extremely delicious not just because of the quality of food but also because of the college type atmosphere that we were able to recreate during those 40-45 minutes.

After lunch, we talked about the molds that I would need to develop. Bansal told me that for the body of your product, you would require 2 molds. One for the front side and one for the backside. However, I was thinking that we should just do one mold and cover the backside with the netting. I knew, developing 2 molds would cost me lots of money and I had no money. I was borrowing money from Sunil and Vijay. Therefore, I wanted to minimize the investment. Bansal though suggested to me that if you just develop the front frame and don't develop the back frame, then, the final product is going to look extremely unprofessional and might not even sell in the market. He then said that let's have a chat with the mold maker too. I asked, who is the mold maker? He said he had also invited the mold maker so that I can meet him as well as discuss the complexities of developing the molds. Daler arrived 10 minutes later to Bansal's Nangloi office.

Daler had been in mold making business for 20 years. Tejpal his partner was also accompanying him. Bansal first settled his payments with Daler and thereafter introduced me to him. I said 'Hi' to him. Bansal started laughing saying, Sachin, we are in the manufacturing business, 'Hi', 'Hello' doesn't work here. Namaskar Jee or just a shake of hand works well. I did shake hands with Daler and Tejpal.

After the pleasantries, I explained my needs to Daler. He was quiet and just nodded his head in agreement. Once I was done with my explaining, Daler too said that I would need to develop 2 molds - one for the front side and one for the backside. I said, OK, I will discuss this with my other partners. However, what would be the cost of developing these 2 molds?

Daler and Tejpal also looked at the Google image of the wall clock that I had shown to Bansal. I also gave them my dimensions including the diameter. Based on that, he gave me a very rough estimate that front cover mold would cost me about 1.5 to 1.6 Lacs and the back cover would cost me around 1 Lac. Daler also told me clearly that these are simply rough estimates based on what I had shown to them. The cost could increase 25-30% if there are changes in the design. Well, 1.5 to 1.6 Lacs looked extremely high to me. And deep down, I said to myself, Sachin, Forget this product. However, I did not show my emotions to anyone of them. I just accepted their estimate. Daler and Tejpal then left. I told them that I will come back to them within 10 days.

Once they left, I asked Bansal, are you sure this estimate is fair? Bansal assured me that he has been working in the manufacturing industry for more than 10 years, and therefore, he assured me that it's a fair estimate. But we can still negotiate with Daler once your design is ready. At this stage, you wanted a rough estimate and you have a rough estimate. Yea, I nodded. Bansal also asked me to remain patient during the mold development process.

I came home thinking about the molds. The cost to develop even a single mold appeared extremely high to me, forget developing two molds. With that rough estimate of front cover and the variable costs for many different parts, I started to calculate the final investment required to get going in this business. I had already estimated the variable cost to be around Rupees 800 per piece. On top of that, the fixed cost required to develop a single mold came to be about 1.6 Lacs. Therefore, I now knew that I needed a minimum of 10 Lacs Rupees to manufacture 1000 pieces for the Mosquiter Product. Moreover, if I add the GST that I would need to pay on fixed cost as well as on variable cost, then, the total amount required would be approximately 11.8 Lacs (10 Lacs x 1.18). So, what I needed was about Rs 12 Lacs. That was extremely high. Sunil could lend me 3-4 Lacs. And then, Vijay is my other hope. However, asking Vijay for 7-8 Lacs would be too much. Therefore, I said to myself, this product isn't happening. No way.

I was damn sure that I can't contact any of my family members. They had lost all hope in me. I was a 'Khali' or 'Bekar' in their eyes. So, talking to my family members won't just be a waste of time but also a humiliating experience. I gave up that thought altogether. And instead focused on influencing Vijay and Sunil Positively.

The next day, I called up Sunil, and I discussed the total investment required to get going in this business with him. Of course, Rupees 12 Lacs appeared high to him as well. He was willing to lend me 4 to 4.5 Lacs. But beyond that, he had no money. He had recently invested in a home in the UK and therefore he was paying regular EMIs. I was thankful to Sunil for this much support.

Now, I contacted Vijay and discussed the total investment required to start manufacturing the first 1000 pieces. I asked him for Rupees 7-8 Lacs on loan. He gave me his reasons for not having this much money. I understood his reasons. However, he was still able to lend me approximately 5 Lacs Rupees. So, at most I could raise Rs 9.5 Lacs from Sunil and Vijay. That was not bad. Vijay suggested to me to start manufacturing 500 pieces instead. I told him, I had also thought about it. However, most of the suppliers would increase the price of their parts because supplying 500 pieces would be too low for them. On top of that, freight cost would remain the same irrespective of whether I buy 500 pieces or 1000 pieces.

Things were tight. Very tight. I again started contacting parts suppliers in China as well as in India. This time, I told them that I won't be able to buy 1000 pieces because at this stage of our business, we are still testing our product and buying 1000 pieces of individual parts would be too much for us. Therefore, we would like to buy 500 pieces. Most of the suppliers responded that even 1000 pieces are too low and if you buy just 500 pieces, then, it will be more expensive for you. On the spot, I took a decision to instead buy 750 pieces. And somehow, I was able to convince all the suppliers to supply me 750 pieces at the same per piece price. And it worked. Things worked this time. I knew I would still struggle to manufacture 750 pieces of this Mosquiter Product with about 9.5 Lacs Rupees. However, I did not want to prolong this discussion. I said to myself, that's it, I am now going ahead to start manufacturing 750 pieces. Even If I struggle to raise enough capital, let's get going. Let's get going to work on this idea. Let's get going and hopefully, the road ahead would be smoother. Let's get going and solve the Mosquito problem. Let's get going and create a wonderful product.

With that positivity in mind and burst of energy running through me, I took a call, Yes, I am manufacturing this product. I had already discussed this product with various people including Sumit, Sunil, and Vijay, and of course my family members. No one else knew about this product. Not even my Mama, not even my manufacturing friend 'Bansal'. Bansal simply thinks I am trying to make an innovative product.

The next day, I contacted suppliers in India as well as in China. I asked them to send me samples of their individual parts. They all agreed. However, I had to pay for the courier charges. The courier charges were high for parts from China. However, that's the cost of testing and is part of the business. Within a week, I had all the parts.

Chapter 4

Mold Development - Phase I
Excitement

Now, I contacted Daler, the mold maker. I told him that I would like to get going with the development of the front cover mold. He said you can visit our office in Keshopur near Janakpuri. The next day, I took 'Metro' to reach Janakpuri West station. Mandeep, one of the employees working with Daler came to pick me. However, Daler was not there. He had gone for urgent work. I was totally mad and couldn't believe that this would happen. I called Daler from his office, he replied, he is sorry, but he had to leave at very short notice. He also told me to explain everything to Mandeep. I was carrying a sample frame that I wanted to use for measurements and angles. Mandeep partially understood my design, but still, he asked me to leave the sample frame so that Daler or Tejpal can have a look at it. I did that and came back home feeling let down. How could it happen that I spend 3-4 hours traveling and still the person was not available?

My impression was so bad that I thought of putting off working with Daler altogether. However, I was a novice in the manufacturing business and could not take chances with unknown mold makers. At least, Bansal knew Daler for almost a decade and surely Bansal won't recommend me someone who is bad. So, I decided to persist with Daler.

The next day, Daler called me and he apologized again for his nonavailability. He assured me that it won't happen again and he will do a good job with my mold. We fixed up the next meeting in the coming week. I visited him again and this time both Daler and Tejpal were available. They had a Tool-room / workshop of about 100 square yards. They had about 4 machines and a staff of 8-10 people. By any stretch of the imagination, the entire set-up did not look professional. It was like going back to the time of the 1960s or maybe beyond. Anyways, we took the stairs to reach Daler's shabby office on the first floor. The office was not actually an office but 8 feet by 8 feet room. There was a computer and surprisingly an air-conditioner too. Daler did not switch on the air conditioner, he simply switched on the fan. It was raining, so maybe the Air conditioner was not needed. In any case, I wasn't bothered about the fan or air conditioning. I simply wanted to get going and make a 3D design.

Tejpal switched on the computer. Daler sat beside him. I sat in front of them. I took the sample frame and started to explain my design to Daler. He understood my design. He is an experienced man and therefore understanding mold design was easy for him. Tejpal loaded the CAD software. I heard about that particular CAD software for the very first time. I knew Catia, SolidWorks, Ideas, ProE, AutoCAD, but had never heard about the CAD software that Tejpal was using. It did not matter to me which software he was using, what mattered to me was that the design process shall start on that day.

Tejpal started to draw the sketch in 2D based on inputs from Daler. Later on, he would convert this 2D sketch into a 3D model. I gave him all the necessary measurements and he was able to develop the 3D model within an hour. It's extremely difficult to elaborate on the design here because it would be too difficult to understand without any sketch. At this stage, all I wanted was a 3D model that would be able to accommodate all the individual parts. The aesthetic did not matter at this stage. I knew I would need to fit various parts including a fan, LED, netting, wire, sockets, switches, etc.

The 3D design was ready as per my inputs. I had a look at it. I asked Tejpal to measure all the measurements. The outer diameter was about 271 mm, the inner diameter of the frame was about 208 mm. The front had the provision to hold the LED. There was also a provision to hold and tighten the fan at the back. There were bushes to hold the sockets and switches. The frame was ready. It looked ugly, of course. It was like a box. No creativity. A design, not even someone born 200 years ago would approve of. Well, the aesthetics did not matter at that stage. The fittings mattered. And with that objective, I asked Daler to 3D Print it. Daler called a 3D printing company and emailed him the 3D model. The guy looked at the 3D model and replied with the price and the time it will take to do the 3D print job. Daler hung up the phone. He told me that it would cost you Rupees 10000 and the front cover will be ready in approximately 1 week. I thought for a while. Rupees 10000 seemed high to me. However, I had no other option but to trust Daler. I replied in the affirmative and Daler called this 3D printing company again to start the work.

I came back home, again, thinking about the cost. The start of this manufacturing journey of mine seemed expensive to me. The next day, I transferred the amount to Daler's account. I hadn't yet asked Sunil and Vijay to transfer the amount. I had some money, in thousands, though. That was enough for me to get going in this manufacturing phase. A week later, I called up Daler to inquire about the 3D print model. The piece was not ready. However, Daler sent me an image of the work in progress. By now, I should have got used to the indiscipline in the manufacturing industry. But I was still hoping that things would be OK in the actual mold development and manufacturing phase. With that positive thought, I set a target date for the launch of my product. I said, OK, 1st October 2018 would be ideal. It was already the last week of July. And Daler had promised me to deliver the front cover mold by September 20 provided I order for the mold by the first week of August.

I was content with that date. I had already talked to the suppliers and all I had to do was place the orders. The work seemed manageable to me. It was easy peasy. I would get the mold on September 20, then, 4-5 days of testing, and then, in 2-3 days I would get the 1000 front cover pieces. And thereafter, I would just start assembling the parts on the front cover. Everything seemed in place. Manufacturing is easy, I thought. And if people like this Mosquiter Product, then, nothing like this business. Bravo!

I discussed the probable launch date with Sunil and Sumit. They were delighted as well. They were of the opinion that, October is the month when the mosquito population is highest across India. It's not too hot in October and Monsoon season has just passed by. I concurred with their logic. October is the month when hospitals are full of patients suffering from Dengue and Chikungunya. So much so, opposition political parties start making catchy slogans to attack the ruling government in states across India for the widespread cases of Dengue and other mosquito-related diseases. One such slogan caught my eye "Machcharo ne kiya Dilli ka Behal, aur bhagh uthe Kejriwal". Kejriwal (Delhi Chief Minister) has run away after the onslaught of Mosquitoes in national capital Delhi.

I was beaming with energy that I would be able to launch the product in the peak season and maybe people would get some relief from mosquitoes. In any business, or for that matter, start-up business, speed matters. Therefore, it was imperative for me that the Product shall be launched by 1-October- 2018. The deadline was almost sacrosanct for me. I conveyed my feelings to Daler and he assured me that all is well and the mold will be ready by September 20, 2018. Incredible, not Incredible India, but Incredible Daler.

It was the 29th of July 2018. I got the 3D print model. I went to Daler's office, again, in the Metro. Daler was not there. I called him up and he asked one of his employees to hand over the front cover 3D print model to me. His employee took me to the first floor of Daler's shady office. The 3D print model was wrapped up in tight polythene. The model actually looked super ugly. Well, that was known in advance. I turned the model around and was satisfied to see the bushes and various other holders. I took the model and placed it in my bag. Thereafter, I took the Metro again and visited the Bhagirath Palace market to buy some screws to tighten the fan, socket, as well as LED on that 3D print model. I had never heard of Bhagirathi Palace in my life. Daler himself had told me about that market when I asked him about buying screws and nuts.

I came home. It was already 5:30 PM in the evening. It was a rainy day. On my way home from the Metro station in Noida, I faced tremendous difficulty in driving the car. It was raining and my car's front glass wipes were jammed. I could barely drive at 10 KMPH. While driving, I kept thinking, I had to fix this. Then, I kept thinking, maybe I will change this car once this product is launched. I was dreaming. Well, that was the only time I thought far ahead. However, I came back to the ground reality and instead just thought of developing the product first.

After reaching home, I did not waste any time whatsoever and assembled the parts in the 3D print model. The parts fitted perfectly. However, the 3D print model was so weak that I could not hang the complete assembly on the wall. I just kept the whole assembled machine on the ground or at most placed it leaning against the wall. The appliance worked well, however, it made more noise than expected. I realized, it was because of the low quality of material used in the 3D print model. Well, that was my line of thinking. I would only know about the sound once the final mold is ready and I am able to manufacture the actual saleable pieces.

At this stage, I was concerned with the fitting part and it was perfect. The next day, I called up Daler and told him that fitting is OK. Now, I will visit you to fix the final design of the front cover so that work on actual mold can start. 2 days later, I visited his office again. This time, I was carrying some images with me. One of the images that I liked was a decorative wall mirror. I showed that image to Daler and asked him to beautify the front cover mold along the lines of that wall mirror. Daler looked at the image and handed it over to Tejpal. Daler suggested that it would be difficult to first replicate this image and secondly it won't look good for our mold. I asked him for his reasons. He said the wall mirror is made of a wooden frame. And a wooden frame adds to the beauty whereas our frame would be made from high-quality plastic, yet, it won't give that wooden look. I kind of understood his point of view. However, I still wanted that kind of frame.

Tejpal started to draw the 2D sketch again. In order to get a similar design as that of the wooden wall mirror, he elongated the outer diameter of our front cover by about 5 inches. 2.5 inches on either side. Now, the outer diameter of our frame was 16 inches or 400 mm. In the 3D print model, the outer diameter was 271 mm or 11 inches. We did not touch the inner diameter. We did not touch any bushes or holders. Just the outer diameter was altered from 271 mm to 400 mm. I did not feel this elongation on the computer screen. The model looked neat and good to me. I failed to visualize that the actual product would look too big. On top of that, the depth of the frame was about 4.5 inches. I couldn't visualize anything. It all looked wonderful on the computer screen. Tejpal took some pictures and sent them over to my Gmail.

I came home and showed the pictures to Sumit, Sunil, and my family members. And they all seemed to like the design. Yea, it looked good to me. I took another 2 days to think through the design. Around the same time, I was visiting one of my family member's house. I showed the front cover images to them. They all liked it. Yea, the Front cover looked wonderful to all of us. I was happy. And with that feedback from various people, I did freeze the design. It was 7th August 2018 and I visited Daler's office again. This time just to say 'Hi' to him. Not 'Hi' but 'Namaskar'. Well, I learned it from my manufacturing friend 'Bansal'. 'Namaskar Jee' is a preferred way of greeting. I like it too. After the 'Namaskar' greetings, I sat down with Daler in his ground-floor workshop or shall I say Tool-room. Well, Daler would get angry if I called his Tool-room as a workshop. The workshop sounds something 100 years ago. Whereas Tool-room sounds more modern. We did not go to his shady office on the first floor. We just chatted in his workshop, oops, Tool-room. I said, my design is final and now when can you start the mold? He replied, from tomorrow itself. He will place an order for the Loha (Iron) tomorrow. I was perfect with the early start as I did not want to miss on the 1-October-2018 launch for my product. Daler asked me for some payments. I said I will transfer some payment to his account tomorrow. He was fine with that. We were basically going on trust now. We will make the bills at the final stage. This is how things are conducted in the manufacturing industry in India. At least when it comes to the development of molds. I, however, did ask Daler, if there are any minor changes to the design in the future, would that it be OK? He said, yea, minor changes, not major changes. I said, yea, minor changes such as placement of bush, holders, etc. He said, yea, no problem in that. However, if you wish to change the design or look or the dimensions, then, it would be too difficult. I assured him that, everything is fine, just some minor changes such as in bush or holders might be or might not be needed. He nodded. And then, he said, I am also going to Mayapuri, I can drop you to the nearest Metro station. I did not mind that.

On the way to Metro station, we got talking about various topics including our common link 'Bansal', 1984 Sikh riots, and politics. He told me that all the areas around Keshopur such as Vikas Puri, Tilak Nagar were developed post-1984 riots. I said that it must have been a tough time. I just said that based on the depth of his tone. He nodded in agreement, yea, very tough times. But things are perfect now. There is complete harmony, he replied.

I got down at the Metro station and came back home. Well, I had not yet fixed the cost of developing the mold with Daler. I was under the impression that it would still cost me 1.5 to 1.6 Lacs. The next day, I called him and said, I have transferred about Rs 20000 to your account. He said, thanks. Then, I asked him about the final cost. He replied that since the mold design is now much more complicated than the simple design that you showed us in the beginning. Therefore, there would be lots of machining and much more iron would be needed. Based on that, the final cost would now be Rupees 2.1 Lacs. I was like, what? But you said, it would be around 1.5 to 1.6 Lacs. He replied, well, the design is too complicated. And I am charging you less because you are a friend of 'Bansal' Jee. I can charge more to 'Bansal' jee, but not to you. I said, well, thanks for that gesture. I said, let me think and talk to my partner and get back to you shortly.

The truth was I had no partner. I simply called 'Bansal' and asked about the cost of Mold. 'Bansal' told me that whatever Daler is charging is very reasonable and if you go to the marketplace, then, people might charge you upward of Rupees 3 Lacs. I said,

Hmmm. I again called Daler and said to him, 'Daler' jee, 2.1 Lacs is too high for me. This is my first mold, maybe you can charge me a higher amount for the next mold but reduce the price a little for this one. He started laughing and said, OK, I can charge you 2 Lacs, not below that. I said I was expecting something around 1.75 Lacs. He said, 'Na Tumhari, Na Meri', let's fix this to be at 1.9 Lacs. I said, OK. So, my first mold will be ready by September 20, 2018, at a cost of 1.9 Lacs. That's it. Everything was in place. I was delighted.

After the finalization of mold and initial payment transfer to Daler, I did not call him for a week. However, I got going to negotiate the terms with other parts suppliers especially the Chinese suppliers. I was under the impression that sourcing parts from Indian suppliers would be rather easy. Therefore, let me now focus on Chinese suppliers. I had already finalized the Chinese suppliers for the uniquely designed fan (8 inches) and uniquely designed LED light. They had already supplied the samples too. All I had to do now was talk to them and understand the payment terms and shipping terms. The Chinese suppliers had provided me the per piece price for both the parts. However, I was clueless about shipping. I had never been in such kind of business to understand logistics or shipping. I was not aware of the terminologies. I was not aware of the 'duty' structure, 'tax' structure, as well as custom clearances. So far, nothing seemed daunting to me, but this one, I mean, shipping or logistics appeared daunting to me. What to do, I kept thinking for a day or two. I googled import-export companies that provide these kinds of services to Indian buyers. I talked to a couple of them. One was based in Delhi and one was based in Chennai.

They asked me many questions such as the kind of goods, the total cost of goods, the size of goods, and CBM. What was CBM? I Googled it and it meant 'Cubic Meter'. I had no idea what would be the CBM of my goods from China. I contacted the Chinese suppliers on WeChat and within 2-3 hours, they replied with all the details. It was coming to be 10 CBM for Fans and about 1 CBM for LED Light. I provided all these details of goods to logistics companies in India. They understood my requirements including the volume of goods I would be buying from China. After understanding my requirements, they offered me the quotes. It was very very high. The shipping cost alone would be 30% of the total value of my goods. On top of that, I had to pay the 'Duty' as well as 'GST and the transportation charges from the nearest port to my Godown in Noida. It all seemed exorbitant to me. However, I had now got going in this logistics aspect too.

I contacted Bhanu and Vijay. Vijay's start-up was already sourcing some machinery from China, therefore, he provided me the details of his TPL. What's TPL Vijay, I asked? Third-Party Logistics, he replied. I contacted this TPL in Delhi and provided my details to them. They also offered me the quote which was also quite similar to what I had already gotten from the other 2 logistics companies. Bhanu provided me the contact number of one agent who dealt in imports from China. Talking to him, I got the sense that this guy indulges in shady practices and therefore no point continuing to talk to him further. I still had no answers to the shipping of goods from China to India. I knew it must be easy because so many Indians buy goods from China. India's trade deficit with

China is approximately 60 Billion USD. That's humongous. Therefore, there would be some streamlined avenues to import goods from China. One week had passed by and I still had no idea about shipping.

Now, I contacted my supplier in China. They were really supportive. They connected me to 3-4 such agents. I started talking to each one of the agents. One of the agents was Indian and that gave me more confidence. That agent gave me a quote of 25% till Ahmedabad port. That 25% included duty as well. 25% meant 25% of the total goods value. That looked reasonable to me. However, I was not keen on taking the responsibility of getting goods from Ahmedabad to Noida knowing fully well that there might be issues as far as crossing state borders were concerned. Even though GST has been implemented, still the policemen do stop goods carriers for some commission. That's too bad. The central government claims GST to be the single most important tax reform in India, however, the mindset of the policemen still continues to be that of the colonial era. Even with all paperwork, they still charge money from goods carriers. I did not want to get entangled in that drama.

Therefore, I asked the agent to deliver the goods to my door. In other words, I asked for the door to door delivery. He could not do that. Maybe in the future, when I buy a large value of goods and I am familiar with the whole logistics process, I might hire that agent to bring goods to Ahmedabad. But that's for the future.

The other 2 agents were Chinese. The language is always an issue with Chinese suppliers and agents. However, WeChat came in handy in that situation. There is a translation tool in WeChat and that helps. The other 2 agents also offered me a similar quote as the one offered by the Indian agent. However, they too were not offering door to door delivery. And I was keen on the door to door delivery. I did not want to take any pressure or risk on myself of carrying the goods to my Godown in Noida. Nothing materialized. Days were passing by. I contacted Daler to check if he has started the work. He replied, yes, everything is on track. Kindly transfer some more payments. I said I will do that in 2-3 days. With assurance from Daler about timely progress, I was now under pressure to expedite the shipping process from China. I was thinking what if Daler completes the Mold and I am not able to ship goods from China. That would be too bad. It was already 18th August 2018. And I hadn't yet found the way to ship parts from China. By that time, I had understood a lot about shipping and logistics as well as the duty and tax structures. However, I hadn't found the agent or logistics company that would provide me the door to door delivery.

I contacted the Chinese supplier again and this time they provided me the contact details of an Indian trader. This Indian trader was based in Chennai but also had an office in China. This trader buys goods from China on behalf of many small traders and provides them with door to door delivery. This trader takes care of all the formalities including pick-up, shipping (fast shipping), paying the duties, customs clearances, and door to door delivery to small traders. In other words, one can relax and not worry about anything related to shipping. However, his commission was exorbitant. I contacted him on the phone. He was good in Hindi. Normally, most people in Chennai would be hard-pressed to talk in Hindi. However, this trader was efficient in Hindi primarily because of the fact that he was dealing with many small traders in Delhi and other parts of northern India.

I provided him the details of the goods that I wanted to buy including the supplier's details. He knew those suppliers. Well, he would surely know, he had been in this business for more than 2 decades and most of the suppliers in China knew this trader. After noting down my requirements, he promised to revert by evening with the final cost. I said, OK, I look forward to hearing from you. In the evening, he did not call, I was restless, I called him again. He replied, sir, give me some time. I will revert to you soon. I said I hope you do because most people forget to revert. He assured me that he would definitely revert to me. With that, he hung up the phone.

2 days later, he sent a message on WeChat. Of course, he too was using WeChat. The message was short. The message included the cost of shipping to my door. It was 48% of the total goods value. GST would be extra. I knew GST would always be extra and that I can claim as input credit during the final sale to the consumer. The 48% number seemed too high to me. During my discussions with various other shipping companies and agents, I had learned a lot. I was now OK with a 35% (25% to Ahmedabad port or any other port in India + 10% for Transport charges to the door delivery in Noida) number for the door to door delivery. However, 48% was way too high.

I called this trader in Chennai. I said I got your quote but it is too high. He replied, sir, I am providing you door to door delivery. Other agents or companies might have given you the quote for LCL shipping, but I am giving you the quote for FCL shipping. Your goods will reach you in 20 days once you place the order. While with other agents, your goods may take 45-50 days. That's the difference in my service, he said with a swagger. By this time, I had understood the difference between LCL (Less than Container Load) and FCL (Full Container Load) shipping. I knew FCL would be fast. Basically, this trader takes small orders from many small traders in India and then dispatches goods in an FCL mode. He highlighted the importance of getting goods on time. I knew the importance as well, especially in my case when Daler is going to provide the mold on time. Therefore, time was sacrosanct to me as well.

I negotiated with that trader for a slightly lesser number than 48%. I said I am fine with 42%. He said, Sir, the value of your goods is too little and therefore I can't go at 42%. I won't be able to make any profit at 42%. If the value of your goods was higher, then, probably, I would have offered you 45%. But at this time, I can only give you goods at 48%. I said, Hmm, and promised to revert to him in 2 days' time. During this 2 days time period, I contacted my suppliers in China and asked about the reviews for this trader. They replied with positive reviews. Moreover, they told me that this is the preferred way of getting goods to India for small traders or buyers. I said OK, then, I will go ahead with this particular trader to get goods to my godown in Noida. What it meant was that this trader would bill me and not the Chinese suppliers. The Chinese suppliers would instead bill this trader. I did not care who bills me as long as I get the bill with all the transparency. With that, I had made up mind to hire this trader to get goods to my godown in Noida.

It was already 21st or 22nd August 2018. To place an order with this trader, I needed money. Until now, I hadn't spent any money except on the 3D Print model and some advance payment to Daler to start the work on mold. I contacted Sunil. I said, hey Sunil, I have finalized everything including the quotes from suppliers as well as from mold maker. Sunil said, cool, so, hopefully, by 1-October-2018, we will see your product in the market. I asked him to transfer the money to my account so that I can start placing the orders. Sunil was fine with that. He did transfer 1 Lac Rupees on the same day and another 1 Lac Rupees the next day.

With that amount, I paid approximately 40% of the value of the goods to the trader in Chennai. With that 40%, the Chinese supplier would start processing my order. I even made a WeChat group, wherein, this Chennai trader and the Chinese supplier were members. As soon as I transferred the amount to the Chennai trader, I sent a message to the group including the transaction reference number. I knew at this stage, all the payments are being made on trust only. I trusted the Chinese supplier and the Chinese supplier knew the Chennai trader well and therefore there was a degree of trust. Make no mistake, the thought of being duped crossed my mind several times. Before pressing the transfer button on the online payment channel, I paused for several minutes. I canceled the payment. Then, again started the whole transfer process again. It happened 2-3 times. Maybe it was a phobia or maybe it was a lack of confidence. Well,

I would put it to a lack of confidence. Years of failure had made me less confident. I still remember, almost 8-9 years ago, I invested a much bigger amount than this in the restaurant business without any fuss. At that time, I always thought of creating a big company. However, that did not happen and at this time, I was reduced with self-doubts about making an investment of Rupees 2 Lacs. Times do change. In my case, they changed for the worse. Maybe if this product does well, and if there is some success, I might gain confidence again. However, truth be told, I was zero in confidence at the time of placing the orders. Meanwhile, Sunil transferred another round of money to my account and the rest of the amount I did manage to get from Vijay.

However, I was still having doubts, 'How can I start this business?', I don't know, 'If I will be able to sell the product or not'. Well, like in life, business is all about confidence, not overconfidence. Maybe 8-9 years ago I was overconfident. And at this time, I was under-confident. There is a very thin line between confidence and over or under confidence. While confidence brings clarity, over or under confidence clutters the mind. I was cluttered, truly, I had doubts. However, after transferring the amount, I thought for a day and thought about just making a wonderful product. I said to myself, at this stage, I need to be an engineer and just focus on making a great product. With that thought in mind, I dispelled all other negative thoughts. I stopped thinking about sales. That's too far. I just need to make a good product. That's it.

With that thought process, I was able to transfer the balance money to this Chennai trader in the coming 10 days' time when goods were ready to be shipped. It was already

30th August 2018. The goods from China were on track. The Chennai trader told me that, the supplier in China will load your goods on 6th September and thereafter it would reach you by the last week of September to the first week of October. That process had ended for me. I would now just follow up with the Chennai trader about the delivery. That's all. With that step completed, I now shifted my focus to suppliers in India. I had already finalized them. One by one I started placing the orders and within 3-4 days, they would deliver the goods. So far so good. I contacted Daler, he would always say, yea, things are on track, you will get your mold 3-4 days here and there than the promised date of 20-September-2018. I was OK with that.

After making the final payment to the Chennai trader, I again sent a message to the WeChat group. This time, the Chinese supplier confirmed that the goods would be loaded on the 6th of September 2018. I was happy, truly happy. Things were going as per the plan. I also started to get the deliveries of parts from Indian suppliers. These parts were wiring with plug, socket, mesh, solutions, screws, as well as other supporting parts. Everything was on track. I now started talking about my product with some others, including a few of my cousins, and uncles. They were all happy, at least, in front of me. I knew I would be able to launch the product on 1-October-2018. However, one thing that was occupying my mind at that stage was the packaging. Oh Gosh, I wish, someone was there to help me in packaging. Not because it was an arduous task, but rather, a boring task. However, I had to do it.

One of my other college batchmates 'Rajesh' was in this business. He was in this business for more than a decade. Therefore, he would not deal with small companies. I was a tiny company for him and I would only place an order of 750 corrugated boxes. However, I did call him, and he was OK to supply me with those 750 corrugated boxes. He asked me about the finished product. I said, the mold is under process and will be ready by 25th September 2018. However, I can provide you the dimensions so that you can start making those 750 boxes. He started laughing. I asked, what happened? He replied this is India, my friend. This is manufacturing in India and not China. And then I asked him, why? What's the difference? He said, you are entering the manufacturing industry and therefore you are clueless. I can guarantee you that your mold won't be ready for another 2-3 months. I said, what? Why? Daler has promised a delivery date of 25th September 2018. Therefore, even if he is late, he would still be able to provide me the mold by 10th-October-2018. He again laughed and said, my friend, put your emotions aside. Just keep following up with the mold maker and don't get emotional or irritated if delivery is late because it is bound to happen. He did promise me that your work won't stop because of boxes. As soon as your mold and sample product is ready, give it to me and I will make sure that boxes are delivered in 2 days time. I said, cool. I said to myself, even if Daler is late, I can still launch the product by 15th-October-2018.

I immediately called up Daler. Daler Jee, 'Namaskar', is everything going well? Yea yea, Daler replied, you will get the mold soon. I asked him again, are you sure? Yea, I am sure, he replied. However, by now, he had already started talking of some extra time, like 4-5 days extra time. I was OK with that. It was already the second week of

September. Goods from China were on the way and they would be delivered to me on time. I kept following up with the Chennai trader as well as with the Chinese supplier. Days were passing by. I also registered for my GST number and within 4-5 days, I got that. My company was now registered. A proprietor firm with a valid GST number and the bank account. That's all I needed for this manufacturing start-up. I did not register for the Private Limited company or LLP. I knew from my past experiences that I can start the business as proprietor first and if there is some sales or success, then, I can switch to Private Limited or LLP mode later on. So far so good. GST registration was easy, I did it myself without the assistance of any Chartered Accountant. I said to myself, yea, things have become good as far as starting up is concerned. At least getting the GST number was a piece of cake. I provided my billing details including the GST number to all my suppliers so that they would bill me properly and I would be able to claim the input tax credit when I finally sell my product to the end-users. Not bad!

It was mid-September, and Sumit called me.

Hare Krishna, Sumit said.

Hare Krishna, I replied.

Is everything going good, Sumit asked.

I said, yea, all is well, things are on track. October-1, 2018 launch date looks good to me. Maybe if not October-1, then, surely, by October-10, it will be launched.

Sumit said, Good! Sumit also said, that's great, you did it. From idea to prototype to building the supply chain to getting the mold ready to final manufacturing, you did it all. Bravo!

I was very happy with that assessment. However, I thought for a while and said to myself, yea, it's good, but that's how things are done, that's how every entrepreneur builds a product. I was actually more happy at the fact that for the very first time, I never thought about the results. In the beginning, sure, I did some market size calculations, but, during the execution stage, the sales or profit never crossed my mind. I was just all into the development of the product, a wow product. At least a wow product from my perspective.

I was now workless for 2-3 days, well, I did not call anyone, nor did I meet anyone. It was all quiet. Supplies were on their way, mold was on its way, and packaging will be taken care of. During those 2-3 quiet days, I said, maybe, now, I can develop the website as well as prepare the marketing material. However, I did not do that knowing fully well that those things are 100% in my control and I can finish those activities in 2 days' time. Well, I already had the code for the website from my previous online business. All I needed was to replace the text and images and website will be up and running. I did register for www.mosquiter.in domain though. Besides that, I thought of preparing several versions of Google Adwords to bring traffic to my web page on Amazon or Flipkart. However, I didn't do it because again it was 100% in my control and I would be able to do that activity in 2-3 hours. It was not slacking, it was a true assessment of work. And once, the final product is ready, I would be able to do a photoshoot as well as video shoot and use those visuals on the website as well as in other marketing material. So, the finished product became very important not just to feel it in my hands but also to develop the marketing material.

But listing on Amazon or Flipkart was an important step and I had no prior experience of listing anything on these platforms. I started to read the seller registration process on both platforms. I also called their customer care and Amazon was wonderful enough to basically send me a link and then handhold me to complete the registration. I was now registered on Amazon as a seller. Flipkart did not show much interest. They wanted me to write long emails and follow a long process and I simply had no time for any of that.

While registering on Amazon, I provided the GST, Bank, as well as business address details. It was rather quick. Thereafter, they asked me to start listing my products. However, I told them, I would start listing in 2-3 days' time when our product is ready. They were OK with that. They also connected me to one E-Comm enabler company as well. That company also asked for product images, however, I had no images. Therefore, they had no option but to wait. It was already 20-September-2018, I called Daler.

Daler Jee, Namaskar, how are things?

Daler replied, all is well, things are going well, give me 4-5 days and I will revert to you.

I said to him. Revert? For what? Within 4-5 days, you are going to provide me the mold? Right?

Daler replied, yea, surely, that's what I mean, give me 4-5 days.

I said, OK. I hope to hear from you on 24th September 2018.

I also called my manufacturing friend 'Bansal' immediately after calling Daler. I asked him about the discipline of Daler. I asked him whether Daler can deliver on time or not. Bansal also told me, this is the manufacturing industry, and things can get a little late. But Daler is good and sooner rather than later, he will be able to deliver your mold. Bansal was speaking based on his experience of working with Daler for a long time. I was happy to hear that.

Now, I started giving the product launch date to many people including my cousins, uncles, etc. I would give them a tentative date of 10-October-2018. They would reply, Sachin, bring the product soon, People are suffering from Dengue and other Mosquito related diseases. I would smile and say, yea, hopefully, this product solves the mosquito problem for many people across India. One of my cousins also suggested to me to patent my product and launch it on a big bang scale. I said, neither can I patent this product because I simply have no money as well as energy to run around Indian Bureaucracy, nor can I launch this product on a big bang scale because I have no investors backing me. Therefore, I would simply launch this product on online channels and if the product performance is good, then, I hope that it will go far by just word of mouth publicity. My cousin too concurred.

For this product, I simply made no elaborate business plans that are taught in B-Schools. I just visualized the problem and the product that can solve the problem. That's it, nothing more. Product development took all my energy. The product development had many sub-tasks including mold development. Mold development was the only bottleneck and I couldn't do anything about this except to follow up and push for early delivery. I was doing that, it was already 24th September 2018, I hoped that Daler would finally call me and give me the good news. However, until 7 PM, Daler did not call me. I was restless, I called up Daler and he did not pick the call. I called him, again and again, he didn't pick my call. I kept calling and there would be no response. I called Tejpal and he didn't pick either. It was a desperate situation for me. I felt suffocated. I felt cheated. There was no response.

The next day, I called up Daler in the morning and he did pick up the call. Before I could say anything, he said, I was in a function yesterday and therefore could not take your call.

I said, is the mold ready?

He said, one of my CNC machines has broken down and we are working on it. We have sent that machine for repair and as soon as it gets repaired, we will give you the mold in 2 days' time.

I asked, when do you think the CNC machine would be repaired?

He said it could take at least 1 week.

I did my calculations, 1-week delay means, he can provide me the mold by 2-3 October 2018. I was upset but I accepted his argument and asked him to deliver the mold by 2-3 October 2018. Daler replied in affirmative.

I knew that supplies from China would also come in the first week of October, therefore, if I am able to get the mold in the first week as well, then, I could still launch the product by 15th October 2018. The launch date was getting postponed. However, all I could do was just follow up. Nothing was in my hand. I could not change the mold maker, it's impossible. Moreover, I had no money to change the mold maker. At this stage, I was visualizing my final product. I said the front cover would be ready soon and then I can just use the meshing to cover it from the backside. However, now, that mesh covering from the backside started to appear rather unprofessional to me. I said to myself when a wall clock manufacturer can provide back cover, why can't I? I also thought that wires, sockets, holders, would all be visible if I did not cover them with the back cover. In most home appliances that I use, they all use a back cover. With that line of thinking, I was convinced that I would also need a back cover. Developing the back cover would mean developing another mold. I called Daler and asked how much time will it take to develop the back cover mold. He knew the dimensions required to develop the back cover, and therefore, he said, it would get ready rather fast and I can deliver you the back cover mold alongside the front cover mold. I was delighted to hear those words.

The next day I reached Daler's office. We went to the first floor. It was afternoon but not very hot. Well, It was 25th September 2018, therefore, the weather was not bad. Tejpal was there too. I requested them not to delay the front cover mold. They assured me that it will be delivered soon. Tejpal again loaded his CAD software and this time I sat beside him. Daler was sitting in front of us. Tejpal loaded the front cover 3D model. He took the dimensions and just drew the sketch for the back cover. I asked him to provide the holes in that back cover in order for the fan air to pass through. Basically, I was looking for something similar to Mosquito Meshing available in the market. Of course, I had not told them about my product. All they knew was that I am building a designer wall clock. I said I need heat to pass through these holes and therefore, I need as many holes as possible. Tejpal made 3 mm diameter holes. I was thinking what if a trapped mosquito pass through this. But Tejpal told me that it would be impossible to reduce the diameter further because of manufacturing issues. I accepted his argument and he made 3 mm diameter holes and each hole would have a 3 mm gap from another adjacent hole. This way he was able to make 100s of holes on the back cover mold. It all looked OK to me. I made sure all the dimensions were accurate so that this back cover fits perfectly on the front cover. I also made sure that this back cover shall not obstruct the placing of the fan as well as sockets and holders. I was basically visualizing all of it without giving any hint whatsoever to Tejpal and Daler. Once the final design was ready as per my inputs, I took another 5 minutes to assess it. It was good. I said this is it. We will make this back cover. Daler said, good, I can place the order for raw material (iron) for it tomorrow. I said, good. And please make sure to deliver both these molds by 3rd October 2018. Daler replied in affirmative again. Daler though asked for some payment. I said I will transfer some amount to your account tomorrow. With that, I came home thinking about the back cover mold. Basically, I kept thinking if all the dimensions were good. Yea, they all were accurate and even if something went wrong, I will ask Daler to change it later.

Now, I was developing front as well as the back cover. I thought of my first meeting with Daler and at that time I was hell-bent on just developing the front cover whereas both Daler and Bansal told me to develop 2 molds. They were correct. Experience matters. They had seen many such products in their manufacturing career and I was a novice. I was basically learning. I had no idea about manufacturing despite being a Mechanical Engineer. It was on the job learning. But so far, no mistakes had been made and I was happy about that fact. There was no wastage of time or money. I couldn't afford to waste any money on redevelopment or rework. Everything had to go well at the very first attempt. That was my line of thinking. I was content about the fact that I hadn't made any mistakes so far. Even the back cover mold is not a mistake, it was a necessity. Although It would cost me some more money, that's another fixed cost. Daler had given me the quote for this back cover. It's going to cost me Rupees 1 Lac. I negotiated with him, but he simply said, he is not going to make any profit in this and therefore there was no scope for reduction in the quote. I accepted his quote and I pressed for a timely delivery. He would always assure me of timely delivery. He even said that he had to stop the work on 'Bansal's' mold in order to complete my molds. I said, Good. Let's finish the tasks soon.

It was already the end of September 2018. I had got some supplies from Indian suppliers. The supplies from China would reach me by the first week of October. And hopefully, the molds will also be delivered in the first week of October. 'Hopefully', I had now started to use the word 'hopefully' a lot when it came to dealing with Daler. I guess it would have been the same with any other mold maker. I again remember the words of my college mate 'Rajesh' about putting emotions aside and keep on following up with the mold maker. I was doing that. I knew I would have to increase the pressure on Daler further if he fails to deliver the molds by the first week of October.

Chapter 5

Mold Development – Phase II
Despair

Even though, none of my family members would be interested in me or my work. They would from time to time call me to inquire about 'what's going on'? I would say, I am just working. On hearing this, they would again say, yea, we have been hearing this for many years now. Well, by my family members, I mean, close members of the family, not some cousins or uncles. I am total 'bekar' in the eyes of my family members. I remember when I was in a job, I was treated like a star and now a 'bekar'. Times do change. From getting humiliating taunts to many other expletives, I had now become cold. I knew, my 'Time will come'. I did not want to prove any one of them wrong. I was basically driven by ideas and wanted to keep working on ideas. I did start the real estate online review portal and it did not succeed. I branched out further in online real estate but did not succeed. And now, I am working on this 'Mosquiter' product and I do hope it gives me some footing. I hope, even if this product is not a breakthrough product, it shall give me some space to work on other ideas. When I talk of some space, I mean, some cash flow. Without cash flow, it's impossible to sustain one's monthly expenses, forget about working on new ideas. Therefore, all I wanted with this 'Mosquiter' product was some space. That's it. If it goes further than this, then, awesome, but I would surely be content with some footing. And I repeat again, I knew that to get some footing back in society, I need to make this 'Mosquiter' product a wow product.

Therefore, I was totally committed to this product. Well, I was enjoying the process as well. Everything was new yet exciting. The only issue so far had been the mold. But then, again, I said to myself, 10-15 days over the committed deadline is not bad either. So, if Daler delivers the molds in the first week of October, then, I would consider it a timely delivery. The weather was lovely and it was the start of the festive season. One month prior to Diwali is truly buzzing in India and therefore, I was upbeat. I even thought, that, if I am able to complete this 'Mosquiter' product before Diwali, then, maybe I can contact several companies and offer them my product that they can buy to gift their employees. With that selling idea, I thought, I could possibly sell all 750 pieces in a few days. Those were only positive ideas. I was making some scenarios. Scenarios to sell the product once it is ready. Later on, I also realized that with the kind of design that I have got for my 'Mosquiter' product, I could sell it in B2B as well as B2C market. Hotels, restaurants, hospitals, resorts would be my B2B customers. With that line of thinking, I started to collect the hotels, restaurant data from the Delhi NCR region. The reasoning behind collecting data was that till the time mold is ready, I can occupy myself with some tasks and collecting data on hotels and restaurants made sense. For the B2C market, I would solely rely on online channels including the Amazon India platform.

I also thought that for the B2B market, I might position my product differently. What will be the different positioning I wasn't sure about that. However, it was now given that I would sell this product in both B2B as well as B2C markets with different market positionings. I still had time to think about different positioning. Let this product be ready first and then I can strategize about positioning. It was the start of October and I contacted Daler about the possible delivery date. Daler did pick up my phone and said to me that 2nd October is a holiday and next week there will be some more holidays and it is difficult to ask the employees to come on holiday to complete the work. I was aghast on hearing this. What it meant was that molds are going to get further delayed. I asked Daler, what do you mean? Daler finally broke his silence and told to me that it would be difficult to give molds in October. I said, what? What did you say? But you had promised a 3rd October delivery. And now you are saying, it would be difficult to give molds in the month of October altogether. This is not right. You have no idea, how much pressure I am under to complete this product before 15th October. Daler said, I know I had promised an early delivery, but you have to understand that this is the manufacturing industry and deadlines are meant to be broken. He further stated that mold making is not an easy task and it takes days of work cutting the raw material, then machining, then polishing. It's a lot of work. I retorted, then, you should have told me at the beginning itself and I would have planned my entire product differently. I asked Daler, please be honest and tell me, did you start the work on the mold when I gave you the order on 8th August 2018? He replied, yes yes, but I knew, he did not start the work immediately and maybe he only started the work on 20th-September-2018. I was wondering, how can he be so callous. Surely, he did not know my situation. For him, I was like just another customer. Accept the payment and promise the date and then later break that promise of timely delivery. This is what he means when he says, 'this is manufacturing industry'.

I did, though, ask him, what do you mean by 'this is manufacturing industry'? He said, things are not at all professional in this industry, we all work without any plans. Nothing has changed in this industry for decades. I asked, what about this 'Make in India' program. The government is pushing for 'Make in India' program and surely things would have changed in the last 5 years. He started laughing and replied that nothing has changed. We work on the ground and we see no change. I recently bought a new CNC machine and loan rates are still high. On top of that, GST has further increased the pressure. I asked, what do you mean by that? He said, before GST, we would do some work without showing it on the book, but nowadays, everything is done as per the book and therefore, there is no margin. If GST rates were low, then, it would have made sense. Besides the loan rates, GST, we also have no support from the government in land purchasing. Commercial electricity costs are very high. Input costs have risen, whereas customers expect us to deliver the molds on time and at a low cost. I said to him. Why the low cost? You can charge a higher fee. He said it is not possible, because, there is competition from China. I asked, what? He said, yea, these days many people go to China and get the mold done in China. Even though that mold costs them twice the amount, but they make it fast and they make it of high quality. I asked, what do you mean by high quality? He said the raw material (iron) they use is of higher quality. If we start using that kind of iron, then, our mold cost will be at least 2.5 times the amount I am charging you. And no one is going to give us 2.5 times the amount. Customers rather prefer to go to China and get the mold. I was stunned to hear all these words from Daler. For the very first time, I was getting familiar with the 'Make in India' program. These were honest words from someone working in manufacturing space in India for decades. I did ask Daler, then, what is the solution? He said, no solution.

I, however, asked him to expedite my molds. He assured me that he is working genuinely on my molds and will deliver soon. He did not tell me the exact date this time though. But he did promise a faster delivery. I was dejected and all my plans for a 15-October-2018 launch were gone. I had even lost hope for the Diwali launch.

On my way home, I kept thinking about the 'Make in India' program. I kept thinking that the government has advertised 'Make in India' so much, but, if Daler is correct, then, nothing has changed on the ground. I kept thinking about the trade deficit with China. It's almost 60 billion USD (4.2 Lacs Crores Rupees). I kept thinking, if 'Make in India' is successful, then, surely, we would not have a trade deficit with China. At least, not 60 billion USD.

Well, on reaching home, I forgot about 'Make in India', but instead started to think about ways to get the molds fast. I thought, maybe I can plan with Sunil and put more pressure on Daler. I called Sunil, well, I gave him a missed call on his UK number. Sunil called me back. I told Sunil, that he should call Daler and pressurize him for the speedy delivery of molds. I gave him Daler's number. Immediately, Sunil did call Daler. Sunil told him to expedite the molds' delivery. Sunil also told him that he is a partner in the product and therefore, the speedy delivery is needed. Since Sunil's number was a UK number, I had thought that it would put pressure on Daler. On the contrary, after the call from Sunil, Daler called me back and said, what, Sachin Bhai, you have informed your partner in the UK, this is not right. If you and your partner put further pressure on me, then, I might not at all complete your molds. I said what? What did my partner say? Daler replied he pushed for timely delivery in very harsh words. I said to Daler, yea, he too is under pressure to launch this product. Therefore, instead of putting pressure on you, I request you to complete these molds soon. Daler replied I am doing my best. I will deliver you the molds sooner rather than later. We hung up the phone.

I again remembered my friend Rajesh's words about 'this is the manufacturing industry'. I called him and told him about the status of my molds. He did not laugh this time, he said, I told you so. I said it seems, molds will be delivered by the end of October. He said it can take 10-15 days extra and thereafter, at least a month of trials to correct everything in the molds. I asked, what do you mean by 'a month of trials'? He replied, when a mold maker completes a mold, he completes it under pressure. Therefore, when 'mold' is set up on the machine to produce products, it gives some errors such as 'polishing is not correct', 'bushes are holding up', 'problems in the cavity', etc. etc. I was horrified to hear those words. According to Rajesh, my molds won't be ready before mid-December. He further stated you would be lucky if you get the finished molds by mid-December. Therefore, he asked me to keep pressurizing Daler for a timely delivery. He told me if you don't put pressure, then, your molds may be pushed to next year. I felt completely dejected. All my goals of the Diwali launch were shattered. It seemed struggles have not left me altogether. With this 'Mosquiter' product, I was hoping for a breakthrough. However, it all appeared bleak at that moment.

Well, to understand, 'this is the manufacturing industry', I asked my friend, Rajesh, 'Is this the norm'? Or am I the only one who is facing this? He said it is the norm. I said, then, what about this 'Make in India' program? He replied, it's only on the surface, scratch the surface, and things are still the same. Nothing has changed. He told me that he still buys plenty of things from China. The things that can easily be made in India, but, we are not able to make them. I asked him. Why? He replied, many things such as interest rates, GST, no support from Government, high input costs, etc. etc. Basically, he listed the same reasons that Daler had listed about 'this is the manufacturing industry'. I wondered, then, why the hell government is not correcting these things if the government is so serious about the 'Make in India' program. Not only will 'Make in India' program provide jobs but also will boost exports. Boost in exports will further bring down the trade deficit and also stabilize the Indian Rupee.

I was not in a mood to think deeply about 'Make in India', all I wanted was to launch my product soon. I guess every entrepreneur is concerned with that objective. Even though I can think through the whole economics behind the growth in the manufacturing sector, most entrepreneurs are only concerned about launching quality products in a given time frame at lower input costs. That's what China is doing in manufacturing space. India can do it too, I said. However, some steps need to be taken and taken quickly. And I didn't want to go into those steps at that time as my whole focus was just to launch the product.

I was now embracing the late launch. Even though, in my mind and heart, I still wanted the Pre-Diwali launch. Instead of getting angry at Daler, I started to accept the reality in India. Maybe I should have gone to China as well and get the molds done there. Or even better, I should have gone to China and hired a supplier there to manufacture pieces as per my design. They would surely have completed the tasks by now. Once completed, I would have shipped the finished product to India and thereafter would have started selling. Well, these were all fanciful ideas, because 'truth be told', I had no idea about manufacturing in India and China. I knew China is far ahead, but I did not know the reasonings. Moreover, I had no information about Chinese suppliers who could produce a product as per my design. I also had no idea about my final design. For me everything was new and everything was designed on the spot. I said to myself, maybe once this product is ready, then, I can go to China for faster delivery. But surely, I could not have gone to China and started this product from there. It would have cost me more.

It was 6th October 2018 and the Chennai trader called me in the morning to inform me that your goods will be delivered to you by 7th October 2018. He also told me that he has provided my contact details to the transport company and they would be calling me to inform the timings. I said, cool, that's exactly on time. You promised the first week of October and you are delivering in the first week of October. Awesome! He replied, Sir, we always stick to our commitments. I thought, how I wish, Daler had also stuck to his commitment. Well, I was happy with the timely delivery of supplies. Now, I started to prepare the space for storing these goods from China. I had no external godown or room. All I had was this rented apartment with 2 small rooms and a decent hall. I knew the goods won't come in those small rooms. Therefore, I emptied half of the hall and made space to store the goods from China.

The next day, the transport company did call me in the morning to inform me that my goods will be delivered after 9 PM. I asked them. Why after 9 PM? The guy said we can only deliver when 'No entry' time period is over. Basically, there are no entry times for trucks and other heavy-duty vehicles and at those times, these, goods carriers can not enter New Delhi. I understood his reasons. He also told me that there are approximately 94 cartons. So, kindly keep the space ready so that we can unload fast. I said the space is ready. I did not go out during that day. I was wondering if the housing society will allow these goods inside the apartment or not. They might object that these are commercial supplies and therefore are not allowed within the housing society. I had prepared my reason that we are storing these goods for the temporary time period because we have recently closed our office and are in the process of getting a new office space.

The goods carrier came at around 11:30 PM in the night. I asked him, what took him so long? He replied that there was massive traffic maybe because of the festive season. The security at the gate of the housing society simply asked me about what's inside these cartons. I said my office supplies. They did not ask any other questions and allowed the goods inside the housing society. The driver parked the truck at the front of the tower. Thankfully, my apartment was on the ground floor and therefore, the job of unloading those 94 cartons became easier for the unloading guys. There were 2 people along with the driver to unload the goods. Well, the driver did not do anything. He simply stood there like a boss and the other 2 guys did the unloading and then storing the goods inside my apartment. It took them almost 2 hours to finish the unloading task. It was close to 2 AM and everything was stored in the apartment. The 2 guys who did the unloading job asked me for the tip. Even though I had paid all the money to the Chennai trader, I still gave them 100 Rupees each to do the unloading job rather professionally. I was happy and also relieved. Relieved at the fact that there were no objections raised by the housing society officials for storing the commercial supplies inside the residential campus.

With that, my supplies were all ready on time. Some of the suppliers from India had also delivered the goods. There were very few items that needed to come. However, I was not worried about those items because I knew those items can be delivered within a span of 3-4 days once I place the order. Therefore, I was confident of getting supplies or parts on time but I was not at all confident when it came to molds. Unless molds are ready, I can't move ahead. I just hoped for the timely delivery of molds and slept late at night. It was, I guess, 2:40 AM or something like that.

The next day, I called up Daler to hurry up the process. He was peeved with my constant follow-up. He did attend my call though and assured me to deliver the molds as soon as possible. He did not give any date though. Now, instead of pushing for faster delivery, I started pleading with Daler to deliver the molds soon. I started using phrases like 'I humbly request you', 'I would be grateful to you' in order to convince Daler about the importance of these molds to me. He would calm down hearing these phrases and would assure me of quick delivery. He even asked me to come and sit in his Tool-room or workshop to oversee the work being done on my molds. I accepted his offer and for the next 2 days, I visited his Tool-room/workshop at 10 AM and stayed there till 6 PM. At least, as long as I was there, work was being carried out on my molds. I did not know if they took out my mold and put someone else's mold in the night. However, I guess, it would be too difficult a task to change molds in the night. Moreover, it would reduce the efficiency of the workforce drastically. Therefore, I like to believe that work was being carried out on my molds even during the night. After visiting Daler's workshop for 2 days, I was certain that work on back cover mold hadn't even started. I asked Daler about the reasons for not starting out the work on the back cover mold. He told me, that back cover mold is rather easy and he had already procured the iron for this mold and he would make sure to deliver both the molds to me on the same day.

I was now in the waiting period. I could not do anything but wait. Meanwhile, the mosquito population had surged in the month of October in Delhi NCR region and of course, I was feeling let down. I was feeling frustrated that I could not launch this product in this wonderful season. Why wonderful? Well, for an entrepreneur, the bigger the problem, the better it is to launch the product during that time rather than in December or January when mosquito population generally subsides. All my friends, cousins, uncles who knew about this product did say to me 'what happened to your product'? I would simply say, it's taking some more time. I had now also stopped giving anyone a product launch date. I would simply say, I am working on it and sooner rather than later, I am going to launch this product. I had hoped for a sizzling Diwali and now I would have to accept a normal or lukewarm Diwali. The buzz had disappeared. And now, I had also started to say to people, 'this is the manufacturing industry in India'.

During my visits to Daler's Tool-room / workshop, I met a couple of other entrepreneurs. They were there to oversee the work on their molds on the air cooler mold-set. I interacted with them and got the same sense from them. In other words, they were also resigned to the lethargic pace of mold development in India. They told me, it's the same situation with every mold maker. It takes a hell lot of time to prepare a mold in India. Not just in Delhi NCR, but across the country. One of the entrepreneurs had actually gone to China and ordered the development of mold there. He told me that he is visiting Daler's Tool-room just to carry out some finishing work on the mold that he had brought from China. He was extremely bullish on going to China to develop the mold. He also told me that you should have done the same. It's frustrating to prepare a mold in India. He told me, that In China, he got his air cooler mold-set completed in about 4 weeks time. And now, he would spend 2-3 days at Daler's Tool-room to provide finishing touches to his air cooler mold-set. I asked him, how much did it cost? He did not tell me the amount, but he told me that for the kind of quality that he is getting from China, it's much cheaper than developing the same quality mold in India. I was stunned to hear those words. I was thinking, I am getting low-quality mold and on top of that, it's taking months to complete the molds. It's nonsensical. I wasn't critical of those entrepreneurs going to China and giving work to Chinese companies instead of providing work to Indian companies.

We hear a lot of rhetoric in times of tension with China. Many people call for a complete ban on buying Chinese goods. There are many messages that circulate on Facebook, Twitter, WhatsApp about why we all should stop buying Chinese made goods. It's primarily driven by emotions. People, in fact, start criticizing the entrepreneurs or businesses that deal with Chinese goods. Well, after getting a taste of manufacturing in India, I can safely say that instead of criticizing entrepreneurs or businesses, people shall, in fact, criticize our policymakers. Why hasn't India able to do well in manufacturing? The answers are simple but our policymakers have been too lethargic to formulate a well laid out manufacturing policy. The labor is cheap in India, then, how the hell can't India be a superpower in manufacturing? In the following chapters of this book, I will list down the reasons for our failure in the manufacturing sector and the steps that shall be taken immediately to revive the manufacturing sector.

Well, the government did launch 'Make in India'. However, on the ground, things are still the same. When I say on the ground, I mean, for small and medium scale industries, things are more or less the same. And as they say, small and medium scale industries are the backbone of any growing economy. Therefore, the focus must be given to these small and medium scale industries. I have been a witness to this situation. It's an insider's view and not someone sitting in an air-conditioning room and preparing a report on manufacturing in India. I know from my own experiences as to what plagues the manufacturing industry in India despite the big claims by the government in power irrespective of the party.

The thoughts had started to converge in my mind as to what needs to be done to lift the manufacturing sector. However, at this stage, I was still focused on getting the molds ready and launching the product. I am still an entrepreneur and will be an entrepreneur. This book is basically meant to catalyze the policymakers. And this book will provide in-depth answers to the problems at hand.

It was already the last week of October, the molds were still not ready. Diwali was on November 7, and I was now a hundred percent certain that I can't launch my product before Diwali. All my plans including marketing plans were put on the back burner. It was disheartening. It can break down an entrepreneur. It can discourage future entrepreneurs. Even my own enthusiasm has hit rock bottom. However, I was now very much invested in the product and therefore there was no chance of backing down. Had I known at the beginning itself that it would take a long long time, then, maybe I wouldn't have entered this manufacturing industry in India. During this journey of 6-7 months, there were moments when I thought, yes, finally, I have a good product. And with this good product, I can set my career on the path to success and hopefully in the future I would be able to launch some other products including the tech products. I would imagine that I can be a real entrepreneur. But the very next day, I will be brought back to the ground by various delays in the development of this product. I would again be resigned to the struggles ahead. One day things look rosy and for the majority of days, things look bleak. This is how an entrepreneur goes through product development especially in the manufacturing industry in India.

Finally, after weeks of pressure on Daler, he did call me to give good news. It was the 2nd of November 2018. Daler said that your front cover mold will be ready by tomorrow. Daler asked me the address where he should deliver the front cover mold. I was happy to hear those words. I immediately called my manufacturing friend 'Bansal'. I asked whether I can send the mold to his manufacturing plant. 'Bansal' replied in affirmative. He asked to send the mold to his MangolPuri Plant. It did not matter to me where manufacturing takes place as long as it takes place. After getting the nod from 'Bansal', I called Daler and provided him the address of 'Bansal's' MangolPuri Plant. Daler knew that address very well and assured me of delivering the mold on 3rd November 2018. I was ecstatic like a school kid. I said to myself, phew, finally, this mold is ready and maybe now I would be able to launch my product within 2 weeks. In that exuberance, I forgot 'Rajesh's' words about the number of trials a mold goes through. I was super ecstatic and really thought about launching the product in 10-15 days. The next morning, I called MangolPuri plant's head 'Kishan'. Basically, 'Bansal' had provided me his number in order to coordinate all my tasks better. I informed 'Kishan' that mold maker Daler will be sending one mold by afternoon. I asked Kishan to inform me as soon as the mold arrives. Kishan said, yes, sure. However, it was already 4 PM and I hadn't heard anything from 'Kishan'. I was getting impatient and called Kishan again. He did not take my call. I called him again and he still did not take my call. I called him 3rd time and he did pick up my call and without any 'hi' or 'namaste', he said, 'Sachin Jee', why are you getting impatient, I will inform you as and when mold arrives. That meant, mold hadn't been delivered by Daler yet. I called Daler and asked about the mold. He said, sir, the truck driver has gone to a faraway location and now he would only come at night and I would now send your mold tomorrow. By this time, I should have got used to the ways in which Daler operated. But I took his words every time he promised something. My excitement came falling down as soon as I heard that mold will be delivered tomorrow. It wouldn't have made much of a difference to my launch date, but it surely brought me down from the euphoria.

I had started to accept that 'this is the manufacturing industry in India' and things will never be on time. However, whenever someone promised a particular date, I would still take those words and begin to plan or rather begin to dream. Maybe if ever I work on another manufacturing product, I will be more accepting of 'ways of working' in the manufacturing industry in India. But who knows, at that time, I may have achieved a little bit of footing in the manufacturing industry and plan things differently for the second product. Maybe I also end up going to China for mold development or even better for the finished product development. But that would be hugely wrong. Given the fact that, India is a low-income country where wages are still low, then, going to China for finished product development would not only be wrong but also criminal. However, unless the manufacturing industry improves in India big time, then, what is the other option left? None! How can the manufacturing industry improve in India when it hasn't improved for so many decades? Why is India's trade deficit with China swelling year after year? All the experts, consultants, commentators, entrepreneurs raise their voice, write detailed columns, and yet, the manufacturing industry is not just unprofessional but also far behind. Governments after governments have promised to revive the manufacturing industry, and yet, things remain the same on the ground. What could be the reasons? These are the questions every entrepreneur ponders over as well. And yet no outcome.

My mind was now totally into the manufacturing industry in India and I would think for long about the ways in which things can be improved. However, I had no plans of writing columns, articles, leave aside the book. I was just bullish on my product. I wanted to launch it as soon as possible and get some footing in life. Or in plain words, make some money. All my energies were on the front cover mold. Even though I wasn't personally involved in mold development, the journey seemed as if I was physically involved in it. Like a tech start-up entrepreneur who does the coding, I was building that mold. I was so involved. Finally, Daler did send the mold to the Mangol Puri plant on 4th November 2018. Kishan called me to inform me that mold has arrived. I was happy and asked if we can start production tomorrow. Kishan told me that this call will be taken by the Boss (Bansal). Therefore, you must speak to the Boss. I did that. I called 'Bansal' and asked about the possibility of starting the trial or production on my mold. 'Bansal' thought for a while and informed me that the machine on which he would have tried my mold had broken down and it will take at least 7-10 days to correct it. He told me that the tentative date to start the trial would be around 13th November 2018. I was stunned to hear those words. I was like, what? Really? But I had no option but to wait.

I called Daler and informed him about the non-availability of the machine at 'Bansal's' manufacturing plant. Daler told me that it would be wise to wait than take the mold to some other company for trials. I asked him. Why? He said, It's Diwali season and most of the labor is on holidays and they will only return next week. Therefore, stay patient and conduct the trials at 'Bansal Jee's' manufacturing plant only. I was resigned to that reality. I had to wait for another 10 days before I can actually see the front cover piece. I was extremely excited to see the front cover piece. But I had to stay patient. Good things take time! I said to myself.

With that, I went into the holiday mood. Well, what holiday mood, I had nothing else to do. Most of my friends were busy in their families and going away for a trip was not at all possible. I just spent that week visiting some of my cousins in Delhi NCR. My relatives came for a day or two. That's how those 10 long days passed by. But believe me, those 10 days were rather tough. The mosquitoes were buzzing with a vengeance, at least in the society where I live. And all those mosquitoes kept reminding me of the golden opportunity that had been lost by not launching this product around this time. In my home, I was content with my prototype, but that was just one machine. Maybe in my home itself, we needed 2-3 such Mosquito machines. The surge in the mosquito population though gave me some positive vibes. Positive vibes about the scale of the problem and the potential of my product. This could become something, I would say to myself. However, I would soon come back to the ground as soon as I would think about developing the product first. I knew how difficult it is to develop the product first. Marketing and selling is another herculean task altogether. Therefore, it would make sense to stay in the present and not get ahead of yourself, I would keep reminding me of this reality. The people who knew about this product would say to me that you are the only one who loves mosquitoes. I would say, yea, the more the better. It's true, no one loves mosquitoes, but for me, they are everything now. I would tell people, I had to develop this mosquito product so that all of you people who hate mosquitoes will eventually start loving me or my company.

Well, that was all chit-chat or a banter. Deep down I knew that firstly the product shall be launched and secondly people shall like the product. Acceptance or rejection of a product is dependent on so many variables, therefore, let me first develop a super product and thereafter worry about people loving me or my company. Even though it was getting delayed day by day, week by week, month by month, I still stayed positive. I still kept dreaming about launching this product. And finally, on 12th November 2018, 'Bansal' sent me a text about the start of trials on my mold on 13th November 2018. The next day, I left early at around 7:30 AM. Again, I took the Metro and reached the MangolPuri plant at around 9 AM. Kishan had not reached the office yet. He was about to come as well. I talked to some workers in the plant and asked about my mold. They showed me the mold. It was round in shape and was about 30 inches in Diameter with about 15 inches of depth. It was huge and heavy. I asked what would be the weight of this mold? One of the workers guessed, shall not be less than 600 KG. I was like, really? This heavy? Yea, molds are normally heavy, he replied. After hearing about the probable weight of my mold, I thought, maybe Daler did not delay it. It's such a big mold, and surely getting it ready would take time. However, immediately, that worker showed me other molds and they all looked heavier than my mold. I asked, what would be the weights of these molds. He replied, approximately, 1 ton. I was like, what, really? So heavy? Immediately, I was back to cursing Daler for delaying my mold.

Kishan now arrived in the plant. It was about 9:30 AM. I was meeting him for the very first time. He is a smiling person and incredibly humble too. As soon as he arrived, we greeted each other and he asked his workers to mount my mold. I thought, mounting of the mold may take 30-40 minutes, but it took almost 2 hours. Once the mold was mounted, Kishan checked for water flow, cooling, airflow, etc. Everything was in order. He asked me, shall we start the trials? I said, yea. He said, OK. Then, he paused for a moment and said, wait, the mold maker hasn't arrived. I asked, is he needed here? He said, yea, if something goes wrong in the mold, then, mold maker can analyze it and correct it here or at his Tool-room. I said, but he does not know that we are starting the trials today. Kishan asked me to call Daler to come here. I called Daler and asked him to come to the MangolPuri Plant. Daler replied that he is sending one of his employees. I said, OK, we will wait till your employee comes. It took about 30 minutes for Daler's employee to reach the MangolPuri plant.

Once Daler's employee came to the Mangol Puri plant, he took some time to inspect if the mold had been mounted properly or not. He asked the plant worker to fine-tune the injector bush. I did not know what they were doing. But they were doing something. Once everything was in order, we readied ourselves for the start of the trials. However, the raw material (ABS) was not properly heated, therefore, we had to wait for another 15 minutes before everything was finally ready. The plant worker started setting the numbers in the controller of the CNC machine. He did set up the pressure, temperature, time, etc. Now, they would close the door of the CNC machine and wait for about 85 to

90 seconds before opening the door. Once they opened the door, they took the front cover piece from the mold. They had used black color ABS raw material. The piece was not properly filled. They increased the pressure again and closed the door of the CNC machine again. After another 85-90 seconds, they opened the door. This time the piece was properly filled and they all looked at the piece one by one before finally handing over to me.

I looked at the piece. It was properly filled. The ABS raw material was properly filled. There were some sharp edges and I asked Kishan about those sharp edges. He said these sharp edges are present in every piece including their own pieces. He further told me that they had to deploy 2 persons to remove these sharp edges from the molded pieces. I said, OK, so this is the norm. He nodded in agreement. My worry about sharp edges had receded, however, I was more worried about the actual shape of the front cover piece. In the 3D model on the computer screen, it looked fabulous. However, the real front cover piece was too big. It almost looked like a pan or even worse like a scuttle. The workers working at the plant too called it a basket or even worse vegetable basket. One of the guys sitting there called it a 'Tasla'. I was dejected with how the front cover piece looked. I was not concerned about what people called it. But deep down, I knew it ain't looking good. Kishan continued the trials and he took some more trials before ending the trials. Kishan was satisfied with the mold. He said to me that mold is running fine. Now, you need to send it back to Daler for final polishing. I said, OK. We can send the mold to Daler. Kishan told me that he will send the mold in the evening. I said, OK. And then I came home. It was a rather long journey back home in the metro. I kept thinking about the shape of the front cover piece. Basically, I was trying to convince myself that it's not that bad. Maybe if I change the color, then, it may look good. I tried various other persuasions but I was not convinced about how this front cover piece looked. I came home and my family members saw the front cover piece too. They also said the same thing. It's too big. I was totally broken. How could I approve such a big front cover piece? I started to say this to myself. Despite being highly effective functionally, I won't buy this product on looks, then, how can I sell it to customers. It looked rather bad. I tried to place the front cover piece at various places including in the bedroom, kitchen, bathroom, living room, but everywhere it looked bad. I knew that the first big mistake has been committed. I was now thinking, why didn't I make a prototype of it before finalizing the mold. Maybe if I had developed the prototype, then, surely, I would not have approved the mold and instead altered the design. However, now, there was no point in thinking about the past. I had to take a call. I could have shelved the complete project altogether or look for alternate solutions.

It took 2 days to think. I did not want to visit Daler's office in a rush. I thought deeply about the front cover piece design. And those 2 days provided me the solution. I took out a hammer and screwdriver and started to cut the front cover piece in order to arrive at a design that I had conceived of. After almost 2 hours of cutting, I was ready with a new piece. Yea, it almost looked different and new. It was smaller in diameter. It looked fabulous. It was sharp. It looked like what I had imagined in the beginning. I was delighted with the new front cover piece that I had cut. I was happy. My family members too liked the new design. So, the design was finalized. I already had the prototype. I now assembled various parts on this front cover piece. They all fitted well and the 'Mosquiter' product was ready. I started using it in my home. It worked well, it looked well. It caught mosquitoes that night. I was satisfied with the final shape and final product.

I disassembled all the parts from the front cover piece and packed it in my bag. The next day, I visited Daler's office and showed the new front cover piece to Daler. He looked at the new design. He took out the actual front cover piece from his desk and compared the two. I said to him, the actual front cover piece is rather big and I do not like it. Therefore, I want to make some changes to it as per the new design that you see. He started telling me that I told you in the beginning that you are making a rather big front cover piece. But at that time you did not listen to me. I said, yea, you were right. He said to me, do you realize how much work it is going to be to make these changes. The cavity, as well as injector, would need to be changed. The raw material will have to be ordered again. It's like building a new mold all over again. I said, can't we do the minimum work and arrive at the final design. He said this is mold development. But you don't understand how complicated mold development is. Therefore, let me think hard about it and I will inform you about it by the evening.

Daler did not call me that evening. I also didn't bother him that evening. Instead, I called him the next day at around 11 AM. I asked him, so, what is the solution? Did you think about the possibility of making changes to the front cover piece with a minimum amount of effort? He replied that 'I thought hard and the only way we can make changes is by changing the injector and the cavity'. The third piece in this whole mold will need not be altered. This is the only way out. I said, OK, How much will it cost to make the changes? He replied I will tell you that in 2-3 days, however, it would be around Rupees 80000. I was stunned to hear that quote. It had already cost me Rupees 1.9 Lacs to develop the mold and now this additional amount. I was totally speechless. I started thinking about my initial days when I wanted to start this manufacturing business. At that time, I had thought that mold shall not take more than 1.5 Lacs. Now, it is going to cost about 2.75 Lacs to just build the front cover mold. On top of that, the back cover mold costing will be extra. In a nutshell, it's going to cost me approximately 3.75 Lacs in total to develop the molds. I asked Daler again, how much time will it take to make these changes? He replied I will give it to you sooner than later. He did not give me the date. But he told me that by mid-December, it could be possible. I said to myself, it's going to January. When he is saying, mid-December, then, surely, it would go to mid-January. And that too, I would be lucky if he gives me the mold by mid-January. Well, I did not waste any time and I said to him, OK, start the work on the front cover mold. I also asked him to start the work on the back cover mold. At this time, he became rather animated. He said to me, do you realize how much money I had saved for you? I asked him. How? He said, by not starting work on back cover mold, I had saved you a lot of time and money. Had I started work on back cover mold, then, we would have to make changes to the back cover mold too. Therefore, I suggest, don't be in a rush to start the work on the back cover. I am promising you that back cover mold is rather easy and when front cover mold is ready and after successful trials on it, I can start the work on back cover mold as well and give both the molds together after polishing. I had no answer. He was basically capitalizing on my mistake. I accepted his argument. I knew it is going to get very late.

By now, I had started to make my mind for 1-March-2019 launch. I said to myself, even if Daler delays, surely, I can launch the product on 1-March-2019. 1-March-2019 was good 3 and a half months away, but, I had started to prepare myself for that date now. I also told myself that once the winter season is over, that is also the time when mosquitoes surge again. So, If I am able to launch the product by 1-March-2019, then, it would be OK. I will accept that. With that line of thinking, I started to calm myself. I had become accepting partly because of my own mistake and mostly because of that phrase 'this is the manufacturing industry in India'.

I thought about my execution time frame. I started placing the orders on August 8, 2018. And if I get the product ready by 1-March-2019, then, I would be able to launch the product in 7 months' time. Maybe it's not that bad. However, I also counted the planning phase including the prototype development, then, it would almost be a year when I would be able to launch this product. Therefore, from idea to prototype to testing to execution will take almost 1 year. That's rather long to execute upon an idea. What if the product fails? In other words, I would have spent 1 year to get the failure certificate. Why can't I fail quickly? Why isn't it possible to fail quickly in the manufacturing industry in India? Why can't I fail in 2-3 months? I won't mind failing in 2-3 months. In fact, most people won't mind failing in 2-3 months time. There are many people who crib about their monotonous job and lifestyle, but, they can't do anything. They can't start a start-up. It takes 1 year to fail. Maybe they know it. Maybe they are smart and already know that it will take 1 year to start and launch a product. Therefore, they stay away from taking a jump in the start-up scene. Maybe that's why India is lagging behind China when it comes to manufacturing. There would surely be many people with ideas, but, they won't start. They won't start, not because of the fear of failure. They won't start because it takes a hell lot of time to fail.

This is a key criterion if the manufacturing sector needs to flourish in India. Otherwise, we will continue to live with the same old story. Large enterprises with access to capital will continue to dominate Indian manufacturing. There won't be any new ideas. We will have to accept regular industry products. A refrigerator will remain a refrigerator, I mean, there won't be any new innovation barring some power saving features. An air conditioner will remain an air conditioner consuming tons of power. Just think by yourself, what kind of innovation have you guys seen in the manufacturing industry over the course of 15-20 years? Whereas we have witnessed a hell lot of innovation when it comes to Tech businesses. Why is every entrepreneur we see today is in Tech business? Why don't we hear about successful entrepreneurs in the manufacturing sector? This is a question worth thinking, not just for entrepreneurs, but also for policymakers. I was thinking about all of that during my frustrating manufacturing entrepreneurship journey.

A journey that started with the idea, then a prototype, then came execution. And execution is where things get slow. Too slow. Whose fault is it? Not an entrepreneur's fault, and now I would have to say, certainly not mold maker's fault too. Then whose fault is it? Policymakers, yes, policymakers. The manufacturing policy sucks. There isn't a visible change on the ground. Things are still run like they used to be run maybe 60-70 years ago. Daler or any other mold maker has no access to facilities including trained labor, capital, land. They all operate in an amateurish way. They mean, literally, all mold makers across India barring the few.

I was now certain that Daler was trying his best when it came to my molds. Maybe he would have delayed someone else's mold, but, from my side, the pressure was huge on him. Therefore, he was constantly working on my mold. But having understood and seen his Tool-room / workshop, I knew that he had no access to world-class facilities. He is simply a contractor who would take orders from customers and then do the cutting at his workshop, then, send the mold for machining to another workshop, then, send the mold again for polishing to another workshop. He also did not have the facility to run trials on completed molds. All of these tasks would take a hell lot of time. Not just the time to load, unload, then transport, but also the waiting period at different workshops. A mold that could have been completed easily in 1 month's time will take 7-8 months. This way, the workforce at these different workshops would also become lethargic and would not strive hard to get better technically. All of this would not only increase the cost of producing an inferior quality mold but also increase the time taken to produce this inferior mold. The end result, an entrepreneur loses. The end result, Indian manufacturing loses out. But who cares? We will continue to hear slogans but very little action on the ground. Yes, very little action.

From mid-November to entire December 2018, I just kept thinking and analyzing the manufacturing sector in India. I had nothing else to do except putting pressure on Daler. Besides, I did work on my real estate portal a bit as well. However, the realty market was so stuck that there was almost no chance of cracking a deal. I did add few properties to my property management portfolio though. However, it was all too little. I had given up on the real estate sector, yes, literally. Maybe from my experience in the real estate sector, I can see it recovering in the next decade starting from 2022 or 2023. But before that, no chance. I took a jump into the manufacturing sector not because of failure in the real estate sector, but, I truly got fascinated with 'Mosquiter' Product. I kept talking to Sumit, and Sunil during those 40-45 days of November and December. They both kept on encouraging me. They were the very few ones who knew about this product. Sumit and I had now developed a practice of talking almost daily. Yea, while on his return home, Sumit would call me from his car. Of course, he used a Bluetooth device to talk to me. Sumit isn't the one who will have a phone in one hand and drive from another hand. He follows rules religiously. During these calls in the evening at around 6:30 or 7 PM, we would talk for almost 40-45 minutes. Thanks to the unlimited calls, everyone talks long these days. And we were no exception. Our topics of discussion would mostly center around my product, manufacturing industry, economy, and politics too.

I used to inform him about the pace of work in the manufacturing industry. He would concur with me as he himself was working in a public sector manufacturing industry. We used to discuss how things can be improved. How entrepreneurship can be encouraged in a big way in the manufacturing sector in India. He also knew the workers' styles of working in the manufacturing sector. We both knew the issues plaguing the manufacturing industry. One such day, we got going in a very charged up conversation. That day, I was really feeling down after Daler's continuous policy of delaying my work. I said to Sumit, I made a mistake by entering into the manufacturing sector. Sumit said things are the same everywhere irrespective of the size of the industry. However, he agreed with me that things shall be faster for startups. He asked me what do you think can be done to speed up the processes in the manufacturing sector in India. I said, now, I know in and out about the processes that the policymakers shall focus on if they are serious about the manufacturing sector in India. Sumit asked what are those processes or steps? I said, for an entrepreneur entering into the manufacturing sector, the first step is crucial. And that first step is 'mold' or 'die'. Therefore, policymakers shall focus on promoting Tool-rooms of high quality across India. The second step is about 'scaling up'. The third step is concerned with the manufacturing industry itself. The industry shall take a leaf out of India's IT sector and learn about presentation as well as sales skills from the IT sector. The fourth step is concerned with the policymakers again. The policymakers shall focus on Skill development programs in a big way. In other words, people shall be trained professionally to carry out technical activities in a manufacturing company.

Sumit retorted that these are all high-level ideas. Can you elaborate more on these ideas? I said, yea, certainly, I can write in great detail. Sumit said, good, start writing then and write a book. You are in an ideal situation, my friend. You have a passion for writing, you already write articles on India's economy, real estate sector, etc. etc. You are perfectly capable of writing your manufacturing story. Who knows it may be helpful to a hell lot of people including the policymakers. There it is, the idea to write had gripped my mind. I thanked Sumit and took a commitment to write on the state of the manufacturing sector in India. That's how this book had happened. So, if you are reading this book, then, it's all due to the encouraging words of my friend Sumit.

Even though I took a commitment to start writing, I still could not start writing from that day itself. I still kept thinking about the mold. I still kept dreaming of the day when Daler would finally handover me the mold and I could start production. I was dreaming about the launch date. I was basically itching to bring the product to market. Even though I had developed the practice of writing, I still couldn't structure my mind to start writing about the manufacturing sector in India. Not because I was worried who will read my book, but because my mind was not properly structured. My mind was occupied with the launch. Therefore, I did not start writing in the months of November and December. Instead, I focused on the product. I started to focus on improving the product further. Some ideas came to my mind during those 2 months. One of them was making a transparent back cover. Prior to that, I had thought of making the white front cover piece and dark brown back cover piece. That contrast of colors appealed to me. But one fine day, I was thinking, how would people see the numbers of mosquitoes being trapped by my product. In other words, if I used the dark brown color, people would have no access to see the numbers of trapped mosquitoes. Therefore, I thought about it and discussed it with Sumit as well as some others. Finally, I decided that the back cover shall be transparent in color. The idea was simple, that people need proof of action, therefore, we need to show them the proof. When opposition political parties in India can ask for proof of surgical strikes, then, it is obvious that people will also ask for proof of trapped mosquitoes in my product. There it was, the color combination of the front as well as the back cover was decided.

Another idea that came to my mind was about coatings that I was planning to deploy on the 'Mosquiter' product. I tested several solutions. I would visit chemical suppliers and ask them for the samples. And with those samples, I did lots of testing and finally settled on a coating solution that I would be deploying in my product. I am not writing about those solutions as those are the USP of my product besides the great design. Sumit and others who knew about this product were very positive about my spirit and my thirst for further improving the product. It's true, some of these ideas will play a significant role in the effectiveness of the product when the product is finally ready.

It was already the last week of December 2018. Another year had gone by without any taste of success. I was hoping for some success this year, but it was not to be. I kept calling Daler and as expected the delivery date of the mold was pushed back further. I had no idea when would the molds be delivered. What started as an October launch was now being pushed to next year. That too, there was no visibility.

2018 had passed by and even though I laid the foundation for manufacturing business in 2018, the structure (product) would be ready in 2019. With a great foundation, great structures are created. I hope, I had laid down a great foundation in 2018 for the success of this manufacturing business in 2019. It's true, I did spend a considerable amount of time on design, air-flow, coatings, color combination, choosing the right suppliers, etc. As they say in order to reap great fruits, we don't do fruits, instead, we do soiling, watering, providing access to sunlight, manicuring, etc. Fruits happen. If the soiling, watering, providing access to sunlight, manicuring are great, we may get great fruits. But without any of these activities, we are damn sure to get lousy fruits. Similarly, my product may or may not turn out to be a good product, but the important steps had been executed well. That gave me satisfaction. If I hadn't executed those tasks well, I was damn sure to get a lousy product.

It was the first week of January 2019. After wishing 'Happy New Year' to all kinds of people on WhatsApp and Facebook, it was time to focus on work. And for me, it was all about calling and Visiting Daler. I visited his office on 5th January 2019, Daler was enjoying the winter sun. He was sitting outside in the open in front of his office. We stayed there, we did not go inside. We talked for about 30 minutes. He showed me the mold and he was of the view that it would be ready in 2 to 3 days. I was happy, however, deep down, I knew that 2-3 days would mean 2-3 weeks. But I accepted his word and came back home. Days passed by and as expected the mold wasn't delivered in 2-3 days, instead, it was delivered on 16th January 2019. Daler had sent the mold again to the MangolPuri plant. I coordinated with Kishan and 2 days later, we ran the trials on the modified front cover mold. The trials were successful. The front cover piece looked fabulous. I was happy, Kishan was happy with the trials too. We took some 8-10 trials and then we sent the mold back to Daler's Tool-room. I came home with the new front cover piece. Even though I already had a similar front cover piece that I had cut from the ugly looking first front cover piece. I did the assembly and it was all good.

The next day, I started to conduct some experiments on the completed product. I wanted to reduce the fan noise. Therefore, I covered the assembled product with the pan that had holes. That pan was very much similar to the back cover mold that I had asked Daler to develop. That pan also had exactly the same size holes in it. That pan was more or less of the same size. I noticed that as soon as I cover the assembled product with the pan, the air won't flow, the fan speed would reduce thereby putting pressure on the fan motor. I was stunned. I tried to provide some gap between the pan and the wall, and still, the airflow will be less. I was worried. I was worried about the back cover mold now. This was the second time when I got worried or felt desperate during the whole execution stage. The first time I was worried or desperate was when I saw the first front cover piece. And now I felt the same. I felt let down by my own actions. I wanted to call or visit Daler right then. But it was already 10 PM. I couldn't wait for the next day. There was uneasiness and it stayed with me the whole night. The next day, I did not visit Daler's Tool-room. Instead, I called him and asked about the work on the back cover mold. He said, he had cut the iron and will start the machining soon. I said I will visit you tomorrow in order to make some minor changes to the back cover. On that day, in the evening, I did some more experiments. This time, I tested the assembled product without the back cover. I would place this assembled product against the wall and as expected there would be less airflow. I would then create some gap between the assembled product and the wall and then there would be normal airflow. I tried this process at least 20 times to find out the exact gap that is needed to get normal airflow and at the same time noise is reduced. Finally, I got the right balance. I knew the dimensions of back cover mold, and therefore, I calculated how much more gap would be needed from the wall. The next day, I visited Daler's Tool-room. He was there in his first-floor office. Tejpal was not there. But Daler also knew how to work on CAD software. He loaded the back cover model. I told him that I do not need these small holes in the back cover. Instead, create a large hole of 220 mm, so that air can flow uninterrupted. He asked so you are going to cover this big hole with SS netting? I replied in the affirmative. He looked at me and said, you keep changing the mold every time and then you blame me for the delay. I said I won't blame you anymore, but please make these changes. He said you should thank god that I hadn't started machining the back cover mold, else, you would have to spend more money on it. He made that 220mm big hole. After that, I asked him to create 4 pins of about 26 mm on the back cover. Those pins will maintain a gap from the wall. The gap that I was comfortable with. Daler did that but not without a taunt. I was now happy that back cover mold had been saved. I was happy that I would not have to spend extra money on back cover mold. With those changes done, I came home smiling. This was the first time when I came home smiling from Daler's office.

Really, those experiments helped me save the back cover mold. I was now more or less certain on the performance of the product as a whole. The front cover looks OK and the back cover had been rectified. It really gave me satisfaction. Daler had told me that he will be giving me both the molds in 10-12 days. That meant, by the end of January 2019. However, as expected, it did not happen. The first week of February had also passed by and there was no chance of Daler delivering the molds. I started getting itchy and would call Daler every day. Some days, he would pick up my phone and some days he won't pick up the phone.

On 9th February, Daler did respond to my call. I asked him, Daler Jee, what had happened? What's the status of the molds? And as expected Daler told me that molds are ready but polishing & logo are pending and molds are residing in the polishing workshop. I asked him, where is the polishing workshop? He responded, 'Mayapuri', about 8-10 KMs from here. I asked him, when do you expect him to deliver the molds? He replied, within 2-3 days. I said, OK, I am gonna call you in 2 days' time now. With that assurance, I hung up the phone. I knew, Daler's 2-3 days mean at least 1 week. 2 days had passed and I called Daler, he picked up my call and without me saying anything, he said, the polishing workshop had been raided. I said, what? Raided? What does it mean? He replied that this workshop was in an illegal zone and the authorities have raided many workshops in that zone. Therefore, the workshop is now sealed. Your molds, as well as other molds, are now locked inside that sealed workshop. I was furious listening to this. My dreams were shattered. I felt hopeless. I felt desperate. A kind of feeling, which can't be described, but it felt like the world had suddenly stopped.

Nothing is happening, nothing is going to happen. However, I said to Daler, I don't believe you. He responded, don't panic sir if you don't believe, you can come to my place and we will visit the polishing workshop together. I said, OK, I am visiting you tomorrow.

The next day, I again took the Janakpuri Metro and reached Daler's Tool-room. We then went to Mayapuri in Daler's car. And he showed me the polishing workshop from outside. Yes, it was sealed. I asked him, what's the way out now? He responded something will happen. I asked, what something? He said, the polishing workshop owner is arranging some money and will sort it out. It's just not your molds, there are 25 other molds too. On top of that, there are various polishing machines that are inside the workshop. So, the owner will find a solution. I thought, yea, my molds are worth just a few Lacs, there are many other molds and the polishing workshop owner's own money is invested here, so, surely, he will find a way out. But that was only a way to calm me. Deep down, I knew, 1 March 2019 launch date is gone. It was getting horrible day after day. I could do nothing. I called my manufacturing friend 'Bansal', and he responded, yea Sachin, these things happen. You are new to the manufacturing industry in India and therefore you are getting emotional. Some of my molds had been stuck for years. So, 'Take it easy' buddy, this is the manufacturing industry in India. I just had to live with those words again.

I was still with Daler and I asked him, why did this polishing workshop owner set-up his workshop here? Daler smiled, and said 'Rent'. He said, if each & every Tool-room operator or workshop operator operated out of the dedicated industrial plot, then, rent is going to be very high. He said, firstly, there are very few industrial sites or zones in Delhi. In other words, the supply of industrial plots is limited. And all these industrial zones are very old and people owning plots in these industrial zones are not manufacturers but landowners and they are leasing their plots at a very high rent. Therefore, a new Tool-room operator or workshop operator has no option but to start the Tool-room or workshop in an unauthorized location. Even the operators who already have Tool-rooms or workshops in authorized industrial plots take unauthorized plots on rent when they expand their work. And over time, they conduct most of their manufacturing work from unauthorized industrial plots and eventually lease out their authorized industrial plot to someone who is willing to pay high rent. Many a time, authorized industrial plot owners have converted their plot into a showroom, banquet hall, service station, etc.

In other words, manufacturing is done from unauthorized plots and authorized plots are used for other purposes resulting in higher rental income.

Upon listening to this, I nodded to Daler, yea, land is an issue in manufacturing in India. Daler responded in the affirmative, big issue.

I asked Daler, why don't Tool-room or workshop operators move to suburbs such as Noida, Gurgaon. The rent at these suburbs could be affordable. Daler replied in negative, 'no contacts there'. I asked, what do 'no contacts there' mean? He replied, see, this mold making business happens through word of mouth or networking. And all of us are networked here. Take your case, you came to us through your manufacturing friend 'Bansal Jee'. Otherwise, you wouldn't have come to us. I agreed. Therefore, Daler proclaimed, we have no option but to stay put in Delhi and optimize our expenses including the rent. Moreover, all these suburbs that you are mentioning are already involved in manufacturing some part or the other for the major manufacturing companies such as Samsung, Maruti, LG. Take the case of Gurgaon, most of the industrial zone there is dedicated to supporting Maruti and over time other car manufacturers have also set-up bases in Gurgaon. Similarly, in Noida, most of the industrial belt has been developed to serve multi-nationals such as Samsung, LG, etc. I agreed with Daler.

Daler further reasoned that even in Gurgaon and Noida, I had once gone to search for a place to set-up my Tool-room there. However, the rent in good locations, nearby locations, was as much as it was in Delhi. If you go further inside these cities, then, you may get some places where rent is affordable, but those interiors don't serve the purpose at all. And since most of the small scale companies in these cities have come up to serve the multi-nationals, therefore, there is very little scope for Tool-rooms or workshops. In any case, the mold making process is the same whether you get your mold done in Delhi or in these suburbs. The money and time taken to develop a mold will be more or less the same. In fact, I am charging you less because you are a friend of 'Bansal Jee'. I looked at Daler in disbelief, on the one hand, he is making my life hell by delaying the molds, but on the other hand, he is behaving as if he is doing some sort of favor to me. Well, by this time, the phrase 'this is the manufacturing industry in India' shall have sunk deep inside my psyche so as to not get surprised by everyday activities.

Our communication on the subject of land was interrupted by the polishing workshop owner. He came and knocked on Daler's car door. Daler opened the door and went out. I kept sitting inside the car. I had no interest in going out. However, even after 10 minutes, Daler didn't come back. At that time, I also moved out of the car and started searching for Daler. He was sipping Tea with that workshop owner at a roadside tea stall. I joined them, and they ordered a cup of tea for me too. The workshop owner said that 'authority officer' is asking for Rs 50000 to reopen the workshop. And he is arranging for the money. Basically, he was asking Daler to lend him some money to bribe the 'authority officer' and reopen the workshop. Daler looked at me and said maybe you can pay the next installment for the molds. I said I have already paid you close to 80% of the cost of the molds. Now, I am gonna pay you after the testing of molds. To which Daler replied, your molds are almost ready except the polishing and logo. So, instead of paying one week later, you can pay now. I thought about it and agreed to pay Rs 15000. I thought, let the workshop reopen soon and let the polishing work & logo work finish soon. With that thought in mind, I agreed to pay Rs 15000.

We came back to Daler's car and drove to the 'authority officer'. I didn't want to visit the authority but ended up going there with Daler and the workshop owner. The officer was bombarding how he had saved the workshop from permanent closure. To which Daler replied, 'nothing happens without your permission sir Jee'. The workshop owner paid Rs

50000 to the 'authority officer' and asked him to reopen the workshop soon. Authority officer agreed to reopen the workshop the next day by 9 AM. With that assurance from the 'authority officer', we all returned to Daler's place. I took the Metro rail to come back home. On the way home, I realized the hard work that needs to be put in to start a manufacturing business in India when there is no need to put in that hard work. All this hard work is simply going into futile activities and not in real activities. I wondered the real activities should have been the selling & marketing of the final product. But instead, an entrepreneur ends up spending so much of his/her time in these futile activities. Thereby increasing the cost and time taken to produce the product. No wonder, people are going to China to buy goods and then start selling in India. No hassles. Buy and sell. However, if you decide to be a manufacturing entrepreneur in India, then, surely, you would have to go through these unnecessary loops.

Finally, after putting extreme pressure on Daler, he delivered the molds on 16th February 2019. That day was super not only because Daler had delivered the molds, but also because I was on the verge of cracking a real estate transaction. However, as had been the case with me, that feeling of awesomeness lasted only that night. In the next 2-3 days, I realized that real estate transactions had fallen away and the molds were still sitting idle at Mangol Puri plant. It was back to basics. It was tough. I called my manufacturing friend 'Bansal', and he won't take my calls. After 2-3 days of living in frustration, Bansal sent me a text saying that 'we will start work on your molds soon'. However, he didn't specify any date. It was all frustrating. Every single day was frustrating. I asked Daler if he had someone else's machine that is idle and I could start manufacturing pieces there. Daler gave me a contact number and I visited that person in Mayapuri. However, I was not satisfied with his style of working as well as pricing. On my way back home, I called 'Bansal' and this time he picked up the phone and said, send the raw material to the plant and we will start manufacturing your pieces from Friday. I was happy.

The next day, I started searching for ABS raw material (Dana) suppliers in Delhi. I called several of them, and finally, I settled on two of them. They both were in Kirti Nagar. The next day, I visited the Kirti Nagar. It was a direct Metro rail from Noida to Kirti Nagar. So, that was nice. I met the raw material suppliers. They gave me a quote. However, I wanted to check other suppliers too. And to my surprise, the Kirti Nagar market was full of ABS raw material suppliers. I met at least 8 of them. Finally, I settled on one of them. He gave me the best brand of raw material at the best price. In fact, he happened to be the largest raw material supplier in the entire Delhi. I had finalized white and transparent raw materials (ABS Dana). White was less expensive than the transparent one. However, I had made up my mind on colors, therefore, there was no way of going back on that irrespective of the cost. I placed the order for about 275 KG of transparent raw material and 300 KG of white raw material. The back cover piece was weighing about 300 Grams and the front cover piece was weighing about 380 Grams. Therefore, based on the calculations including the wastage calculation, I placed the order for 275 KG of transparent and 300 KG of white raw material. That supplier asked me for the documents such as GST registration and I provided that. I transferred the money online and on the same day itself, they delivered the raw material to the Mangol Puri plant. The entire process of finding and finalizing the raw material supplier took 2 days. 2 days of non-stop action. But I was happy that it was done too.

I called 'Bansal' and informed him that raw material had been delivered at the Mangolpuri plant. He promised me that manufacturing will finally start on Friday. Friday was 1 March 2019. I thought, maybe I would be able to launch the final product by 10th March or 17th March. I guess that was a big problem with me, I would always start visualizing the launch date without considering the variables. However, I thought, what could go wrong this time? I thought, I thought hard and I was certain that nothing could go wrong. The molds have been tested and therefore, there won't be any problem.

It was March 1st, 2019 and I reached the Mangolpuri Plant at 10 AM. Kishan had also arrived. I met Kishan and he showed me the loading of front cover mold on the CNC machine. It took them another 2 hours to properly load or mount the mold on the CNC machine. The workers now loaded the white raw material for the front cover piece. At one shot, they filled the tank with 75 KG of white raw material. The machine was heating up. The front cover mold had already been tested and therefore there was no need for Daler or his staff member to be present there. It was about 2 PM. After finishing lunch, the CNC operator started the work of manufacturing front cover pieces. He made sure that all the numbers in the control panel were accurate. Having done the check, he pressed OK and closed the door of the CNC machine. After about 90 seconds, he opened the door and took out the semi-filled front cover piece. It was a waste. He tried 2-3 times before finally getting the fully filled front cover piece. It looked marvelous in the white. I guess the quality of the material that I had chosen played its part in getting a marvelous looking piece. Everyone present there at the Mangolpuri plant was awestruck as they had not seen such a high-quality piece before. They all were used to seeing recyclable PP material and therefore the quality of the piece that they used to see was not great. My front cover piece simply looked fabulous. I was in love. It was so awesome that all the workers present there asked me for the final product whenever it was ready. I promised them that I will give each and everyone a finished assembled product.

However, my joy was short-lived, the CNC machine started producing some sort of black spots on the front cover pieces. I asked Kishan what's that? He said, this CNC machine has always been operated on black color raw material, and therefore, it is likely that some of it may have remained in the pipe and it gets mixed up with the white raw material. I was concerned. However, after about 8-10 such pieces, the new pieces were again coming up absolutely clean without any mark or stain. I asked Kishan, what could be done with these 8-10 pieces? He said you can get a white spray and cover these black spots with that spray. I said, OK, at least there is a solution. It was already 4 PM, I went for lunch at a nearby Dhaba. However, they all had closed down for lunch. I saw a shady looking shop that was making noodles. I visited that shop and ate a plate of noodles. It was not hot. But it was in the open. And it cost me just Rupees 10.

After my so-called lunch, I sat at the Mangolpuri plant for another 2 hours. Thereafter Kishan told me that everything is going well now, you can leave and come back tomorrow for the back cover mold. I asked how long will the work continue on this front cover mold? Kishan told me that as long as all the raw material is finished. I asked how much time it would take to finish all the raw material? Kishan made some calculations and told me that it will get over by 9 or 10 AM the next morning. That meant another 14-15 hours. With that assurance, I came back home. I was satisfied. Truly satisfied! I did not call Kishan and I was hoping that nothing will go wrong now and I will get approximately 750 pieces of front cover tomorrow.

The next day, I reached at 10 AM again. It was the first week of March and therefore the weather was awesome. There was no problem going in a Metro or walking or taking an Auto. It was pleasant. I was thinking, had I executed all these activities in summer, then, surely, I would have been 100 times more frustrated. Deep down I felt grateful that all my major tasks had been executed in the months of November to March. That was truly a delight. It did not feel too bad traveling every day so far from Noida. The weather was supportive. The winter season was supportive.

Kishan was already there at the plant. He was in an animated conversation with the CNC operator. I asked them, is everything right? They looked at me and told me that the front cover mold had broken at around 11 PM Yesterday night. And since then, the CNC machine had been lying idle. I was stunned to hear that. I never ever thought that the mold would break down. They showed me the broken mold. The CNC machine operator told me that basically an injector pin got stuck in the cavity and while removing it, it created a dent in the cavity as well as in the main part of the mold. I was devastated. I asked how many pieces were produced until 11 PM. He said, about 380 pieces. I asked about how much white raw material is still available? He said, approximately, 125 KG is available and 175 KG is finished. I realized that loading and unloading of mold not only takes time but also wastes the raw material. It was an expensive process. I started getting angry on Daler and wondered how could he produce such a bad mold. Kishan came next to me and calmed me down saying that these things happen in the manufacturing sector. He also told me that they are now going to load the back cover mold. I said, OK. Kishan asked me to call Daler or his staff member to oversee the loading or mounting of the back cover mold. I called Daler and told him about the front cover mold. He didn't feel guilty and instead said, these things happen. Then, I asked him to send one of his staff members to oversee the loading or mounting of the back cover mold. He said, yea, my employee will reach within 30 minutes. We kept waiting and Daler's staff member came 1 and a half hours later. Kishan was getting impatient. He was more worried about the CNC machine idle time. And I was more worried about the wastage and the cost that I would have to incur because of this wastage. I started calculating the price per piece for the front cover. It kept on increasing. I hoped this won't happen to me again in the back cover mold.

Daler's staff member and CNC machine operator took the time to properly load the back cover mold. It was already 1 PM. They then broke out for lunch. I did not go anywhere. I kept waiting for the operations to start again. At around 2 PM, the CNC operator in the presence of Daler's staff member started the manufacturing of back cover pieces. He closed down the door and after about 85 seconds, he opened the door and took out the back cover piece. It was fully filled and it came out without any problem. I was happy. The color was not fully transparent because they had just finished making white front cover pieces. He ran another trial and again it was a good piece. This time, the color was much better. The CNC operator and Daler's employee told me that after about 7-8 pieces, they would start getting the natural transparent back cover. I said OK. They kept running the trials. And every time a fully filled piece will come out. Daler's staff member said that everything is fine now and he would take front cover mold with him to the Toolroom. Everyone was OK with that. Daler's staff member called the mini truck. The truck was supposed to come in 15 minutes. Meanwhile, the CNC machine operator kept running the trials on the back cover mold. After about 10 pieces, he suddenly looked perplexed. I went there to see the CNC machine. And I saw that the back cover piece had got stuck in the cavity. The CNC machine operator tried to remove it, but he was unsuccessful. Daler's employee came and tried to remove the back cover piece from the cavity too. He was unsuccessful too. Thereafter, he went inside the machine and took a fire rod to heat the area where the back cover piece was stuck. After heating it fully, he then inserted a pin and waited for a minute to cool it down. After that, he started to pull the back cover piece. And he was successful in removing the back cover piece. I asked what was the problem? Why did the back cover piece got stuck in the cavity? He told me that 2 of the 4 pins that are about 26 mm long had got stuck. After removing the back cover piece, the CNC machine operator again ran the trials. This time too the back cover piece got stuck in the cavity. It was the same problem. Daler's employee again went inside the CNC machine and repeated the process to take out the back cover piece. By doing all these manual exercises, I could see some scratches were beginning to come on the back cover mold. The final finish won't be as awesome as I had imagined. The CNC machine operator again ran the trials after spraying the mold oil and this time too the back cover piece got stuck. I was frustrated, everyone was frustrated including Daler's staff member. He asked the CNC operator to unload the back cover mold too. I asked what had happened. He said that they have to polish these pins so that they don't get stuck in the cavity. I was dejected but I had no other choice. Daler's staff member took both the molds back to the Tool-room. I thought, what a waste of time and raw material. I knew that Daler would easily take 1-2 weeks to rectify the molds and then my friend 'Bansal' would take another week to start manufacturing. It was tough, very tough. I knew that the month of March is gone in this trial exercise. I was extremely frustrated.

I came home dejected. My hopes of launching the product in the month of March were dashed. Completely dashed. Daler had no guilty feeling. Instead, he would only say that 'this is manufacturing industry' and mold making, as well as mold trials, take time. But once the trials are done, then, you can just start manufacturing pieces. I retorted I do not see it happening anytime soon. He replied we are trying our best. I again had no other option but to stick with Daler. A week later, surprisingly, he called me to inform me that back cover mold is fixed. I asked, what about the front cover mold? He replied that it is going to take time. Therefore, he sent the back cover mold again at Mangolpuri plant. Kishan called me a day later to inform me that trials will start on back cover mold tomorrow. I was pleasantly surprised by the gestures shown by Daler and Kishan. I was wondering what had changed that these guys are calling me on their own.

I reached the Mangolpuri plant the next day at 10 AM. The CNC machine operator was mounting or loading the back cover mold on the CNC machine. Daler's staff member too came at around 11 AM. At around 12:30 PM, the mold was ready for the trials. CNC machine operator closed the door of the CNC machine and after 85 seconds, he opened the door again. I was expecting a fully filled piece like the last time. However, it was a semi filled piece. But the good thing was that it didn't get stuck in the cavity. We were hopeful that this time the back cover piece won't get stuck in the cavity. The CNC machine operator ran another trial. This time too, a semi filled piece came out. Another trial and same result. The 4th time, we got the fully filled piece. I was happy. He continued to run the trials and every single time, fully filled pieces would come out with better quality. We all thought, that the problem had been completely fixed and we can now start manufacturing the back cover pieces. However, again, our euphoria was short-lived. After about 10-12 trials, the back cover piece started to get stuck in the cavity. Daler's staff member looked at the problem. He went inside the CNC machine and this time heated the large pin that was meant to hang the final Mosquiter product on the wall. This pin is similar to what we see in the wall clocks. After much effort, he was able to remove the back cover piece from the cavity. Another trial and same problem. Daler's staff member was frustrated too. He again asked the CNC machine operator to unload the back cover mold. I asked, what's the problem this time? He replied that polishing needs to be done comprehensively. With that, he took the mold back to the Tool-room. We were all dejected. I was dejected because of wastage of raw material as well as time. Kishan was more dejected because of machine idle time. The only person who was not dejected was Daler. According to him, it happens, after all 'this is the manufacturing industry', I was now beginning to lose patience. I asked Kishan and my manufacturing friend 'Bansal' if there is another mold maker who can rectify the errors in my molds? They both advised me to stick with Daler. 'Bansal' also told me that for the next 2-3 weeks, his machine will be fully occupied. What it meant was that I shall look for another manufacturing job working company that can carry out trials as well as manufacture my pieces. I had no idea about job working companies. I asked them if they knew anyone. Kishan gave me a contact number and I contacted that person. The person sounded extremely professional. I fixed up a meeting with him 3 days later. His manufacturing set-up too was based in Mangolpuri but in Phase 1. 'Bansal's' manufacturing plant was based in Mangolpuri Phase 2.

3 days later, I met the owner of this job working company. His name is 'Garg'. He assured me that he will produce my pieces and also run the trials. He gave me a very reasonable price of doing all those activities. He also assured me that he can provide me full support in the transportation of molds as well as finished pieces. That was a big relief for me. I felt like, finally, I have met someone with whom I can work for a long long time. I felt, wow, here is a professional guy in this unprofessional manufacturing industry in India. I felt light.

On 19th March 2019, the owner of this new job working company 'Garg' picked up both my molds from Daler's Tool-room. He also picked up the raw material from 'Bansal's' manufacturing plant. Everything was now at Garg's place. He had set the back cover mold for trials. I reached his plant the next day early in the morning. The CNC machine operator at Garg's job working company had perfectly loaded the back cover mold on the CNC machine. Daler's staff member did not come. I was so frustrated with Daler that I did not care whether someone from his side came or not. We started the trials. The first piece was semi filled. The second piece too was semi filled. After about 5-6 trials, we finally got a fully filled piece. That was a big relief. However, I was cautious as I knew the mold can still give problems. And that is exactly what happened. After exactly 12-13 trials, the same problem resurfaced again. The pins would get stuck in the cavity. Garg called an expert and he looked at the problem. That expert suggested to Garg to call the polishing guy and fix the problem right there at Garg's place. However, the polishing guy was busy somewhere else. He promised to Garg that he would come by 6 PM. Garg told me to not get worried. He told me that he will make sure that the back cover mold is fixed today so that production can start. However, he also advised me to complete my other tasks. With that assurance, I came back. The next day, I called Garg and he told me that polishing guy had come and he did the polishing for about 2 hours. Thereafter, the mold ran fine for some time before giving the same problem again. Garg then asked me to send the mold back to Daler. I accepted his suggestion and the back cover mold was again sent back to Daler. I was calculating all the losses that I was making in transportation, wastage of raw material, cost of using the CNC machine for trials. On top of that, the mold was going to get damaged and the end result would be a slightly inferior quality of production pieces. That was worrisome. I conveyed my feelings to Daler. His argument remained the same, 'this is manufacturing industry'.

However, this time he did accept that he would adjust some of these losses in the cost of molds.

On around 29th March 2019, Daler sent the Back cover mold again. I asked him, what changes he had made? He replied he had provided 4 injectors that will make sure that mold will not get stuck in the cavity. The next day, we ran trials at Garg's place. Garg had called the same expert again. As soon as we started the trials, we knew this time that there won't be any problems. The expert too was satisfied with the changes that Daler had made. We kept on running trials until we reached a stage where we were certain that this mold is completely fixed.

Garg promised me that they will use all the raw material for back cover mold and finish the task by 31st March morning. It was Sunday. Garg called to inform me that 665 pieces of back cover had been produced. I was happy. I was hoping for about 750 pieces. However, I knew that this back cover mold had been put on trials for 3-4 times and therefore wastage was going to be high. Garg asked me for shipping details. I provided him all the details including the GST, Delivery Challan, E-way Bill. He then sent the mini truck to my address. By the evening, back cover pieces were with me. I had already gotten some 385 front cover pieces from Bansal's manufacturing plant. So, now, everything was ready. I was ready for assembly. Awesome!

Chapter 6

Assembly and the start of the selling process

I spent the next 2-3 days in aggregating all the minor parts required for assembly. Those minor parts were screws, logo, warranty booklet, tools. Things were finally ready. I started assembling and all my calculations about assembly came wrong. I had thought that assembling 1 product may take about 20-25 minutes. However, it took me 45 minutes. Assembling included removing the sharp edges from both front and back cover pieces. Then, tightening the SS netting in the back cover. Thereafter, I would tighten the LED light along with the driver. And after that, I would tighten the fan. Then I would wire all the parts in one common socket and screw that socket in the bush. Thereafter, I would coat the front cover with the coating solution that I had prepared for the Mosquiter product. And then I would screw the back cover on the front cover. The last step in the assembly line was the packaging. All of it took time.

The next day, Of course, I did not do all the activities in a single stretch to produce one product. Instead, I focused on completing 2-3 activities for many pieces. The next day, I completed another 2-3 activities and this way, I was able to bring down the assembly time to 35 minutes. That was a good saving. I also knew that if 5-6 people are working in the assembly line, then, the assembly time may reduce to 25-30 minutes. I was happy with that timing. 25 minutes to assemble a single product. However, till the time, I am in a position to hire 5-6 people, I would have to live with 35 minutes to assemble a single product.

I continued assembling for 10 days and was able to assemble about 50 pieces. 5 pieces a day. However, I had not yet started marketing and selling. After assembling 50 pieces, I started telling some people who did not know about this product. One of them was so positive that he ordered 2 products immediately. After about 3-4 days, I took a single product to his home. He had promised to pay me. I gave him the demo and he was excited by my product. He really liked the product. I had dinner at his home. However, he did not pay me for the product. He said, oh, I don't have change. Can I make an online payment? I said, yea, please do it. I need this payment for 3-4 reasons. Firstly, this is my first order and I am giving you a discount on it. Secondly, I need to pay GST on it. Thirdly, I will feel encouraged that the sales process had started. And lastly, if I am able to sell 100-200 products, then, I may need bills as well as proofs of payment to approach a venture capital fund or banks for a loan. However, that person did not transfer the money. I felt truly bad. I followed up but no success. I will, however, get this payment come what may.

This whole experience dented my belief that I can easily sell 100-200 products in a given housing society. I stopped that channel of sales altogether. I listed my product on Amazon. And of course, Sunil and Sumit were the first 2 customers. Sales had started. However, I did not start any advertising because it was already May. And when humans can't tolerate the 45 degrees C temperature, then, how the hell mosquitoes will tolerate that?

I started waiting for the month of May to pass and thereafter I can start advertising in Mumbai, Pune region when Monsoon arrives. I was primarily going to depend on Google Adwords for advertising. Besides, Google Adwords, I may also run Facebook campaigns to target NRI audience who may buy this product for their parents living in India. I had also thought of selling this product in the B2B Category. In the B2B category, I intend to target guest houses, resorts, restaurants, builders. But I knew B2B is not easy and it takes time to get sales through B2B. So at the start, I would have to rely on B2C by primarily selling on Amazon. However, I had to wait for the Monsoon season to kickstart.

It was already the end of May 2019. I had sold about 10 pieces without much marketing. But on those 10 pieces, I faced issues with Amazon pick-up service as well as final delivery service. As soon as the customer placed an order, I will get a notification. I will log in to the seller central platform and schedule the pick-up of the order. I will then print the label along with the bill and paste them on the package. Since all these first 10 orders from my known sources, I knew, if something goes wrong in pick-up or delivery, it won't impact my brand reputation. I was already concerned about brand reputation. I was of the view that even if the product is good, but if it is not delivered perfectly, then, it creates a bad impression of the product and the company. And at the start of my business, I would never want it. In fact, I would never want it during any phase of the business. For the first order, it was ordered by Sunil, the pick-up guy called me before coming. Basically, he wanted to confirm the address. I provided or rather confirmed the pick-up address. The pick-up guy came and he was in a hurry. Since it was my first time, I hadn't attached the bill on the package. He was mad. He didn't even want to wait for a minute. I hurriedly attached the bill on the package and handed over the package to him. He scanned the barcode and took the package. I logged into the seller central and the status of that order changed from 'waiting for pickup' to 'picked up'. It was satisfactory, the first order had been dispatched. Within 2-3 days, it was delivered to Sunil's home. Sunil called me from the UK to confirm that the package had been received and it was all good. I was happy that there were no issues in the delivery. I thought, wow, it ain't bad. My next order was placed by Sumit. I scheduled its pick-up for the next day. However, no one came to pick the order. I registered a case with Amazon and asked them to send someone to pick up the order. But 2-3 days had passed by and no one came to pick up the order. I was aghast, I reopened the case and pressurized them to pick up the order. They promised me that within 24 hours someone will come and pick up the order. I said to myself, my gosh, this is unprofessional and if this continues, then, selling on Amazon would be tough. The next day, Sumit called me early in the morning at around 6 AM. Sumit said, hey, Amazon has canceled the order and they are going to refund the money. I was horrified to hear that. Sumit also knew that I had scheduled the order but Amazon pick up guy did not come for so many days. I registered another case and this time blasted the Amazon seller support team for their unprofessional attitude. They called me from their headquarters and asked for the issue in detail. I gave all the details to them. They promised me that they will appoint a new pick-up guy for my region. With that assurance, I hoped for better service.

Sumit placed the order again. This time, the pick-up guy came on time and took the package. The new person was polite and seemed professional. I was happy with the change in the person. 2-3 days down the line, Sumit called me again. This time, Sumit blasted me. Sumit shouted I told you that you need to provide high-quality packaging in order to make sure that the product is not damaged. He sent me the images of the damaged product. It was horribly damaged. Sumit told me that with the kind of packaging you are providing, any product will get damaged because the logistics guy simply throws around packages during the whole delivery process. They are all in a hurry. So, you need to provide perfect cushioning. No matter, you are using high-grade ABS material in your product, but you need to provide extra cushioning in order to make sure that the product is not damaged during delivery. I understood his point. The next day, Sumit came to my house and I replaced his product. Well, I could have provided him the product from my home in the first instance, but I wanted to test Amazon pick up and delivery process. And truth be told, I was disappointed with Amazon pickup and delivery service. However, I understood Sumit's point as well about providing extra cushioning. The next day, I went to the packaging manufacturing plant and bought a roll of 4 mm foam. For my next orders, I started to wrap the product in this foam. And this was helpful. The next few orders were delivered on time and without any damage. Even though the extra cushioning raised the cost, but deep down, I knew that it's better than getting customer returns. With those first 10 orders from known sources, I was able to sort out Amazon pickup and delivery service. It took almost a month to sort out this process. But, it was finally sorted out. I would now be not worried about pick up and delivery at all. The packaging was sorted out as well. This is what we call as 'on the job learning'. Well, in this manufacturing journey of mine, everything had been an 'on the job learning'.

Southwest Monsoon had arrived in India. It was the first week of June 2019. Based on the Indian Meteorological Department data, I came to know about the delays in Monsoon. Monsoon was now supposed to hit Mumbai region in the second to the third week of June 2019. Monsoon season was important for me as this is the time when mosquito population surges. I wanted to make sure that I promote my product on a variety of platforms during this Monsoon season. And Mumbai is a metro city and getting traction in Mumbai city would catapult my product into instant fame. That was my line of thinking. Or shall I say, dream? However, I was constrained by resources. I did not have the resources to promote my product on a variety of platforms in Mumbai city. Therefore, I narrowed down the channels to just Amazon sponsored products and Google Adword. I was familiar with Google Adword, and learning Amazon sponsored products was a piece of cake for me. I started with a daily budget of Rupees 100 on both these platforms. I started to get some clicks. However, sales did not happen. 2 weeks had passed by, but no sales happened. I was getting restless. I thought deep and long about the whole strategy. I had an Amazon landing page, i.e. my product page. I was using Amazon Sponsored product as well as Google Adword to bring clicks or rather say traffic to my product page. What's wrong? Why aren't people buying? Is price the main deterrent? Is product positioning wrong? Or people simply don't buy new brands? I kept analyzing all these questions. I had no concrete answer. What if I change the positioning? What if I change the price? But, I did not change those things as I simply had no data. However, I did put as much information as possible on the Amazon product page including the benefits, features, installation, and high-quality pictures. I even sat with Sumit for good 2-3 hours to finetune the product description and product features. However, sales did not happen. I even made videos including 'how to install', 'how it works', 'benefits', etc. But getting eyeballs on those videos as well as on Amazon product page was a herculean task. Maybe I need to utilize the offline advertising channels, I said to myself. But that thought quickly evaporated given the costs involved in offline advertising channels.

Finally, on June 24, 2019, I had my first order. First genuine sale. The previous 10 sales were from known sources. This one was a genuine customer. And yes, this customer was from Mumbai. I was excited. I thought, maybe this is the start of the cycle. I dispatched the package and there was no issue whatsoever in pick-up and delivery. I was now 100% certain that pick-up and delivery are perfectly fine-tuned. After a week's time period, I logged into seller central platform and asked for the review from this customer. To which the customer simply replied to my question, stating 'works well'. However, this customer did not write a review. I did not want to push this customer further in writing a review. I knew that reviews are important to boost online sales. I had already gotten 3-4 reviews from the previous 10 sales. But 3-4 reviews are not enough to start ranking higher in the category that I was selling into. I wanted at least 15 reviews by the end of June 2019. But I had only 3. Sales were not happening and therefore what are the other ways to get reviews? None! I did not want to buy reviews. So, I kept on advertising on Amazon sponsored products and Google Adword to generate traffic hoping it will lead to sales and then a few of those customers would provide genuine reviews.

The month of June 2019 had passed by with only one genuine sale. I was not disappointed, I thought, maybe that's how things work in the beginning. Thinking and planning on a daily basis, I knew, I couldn't rely solely on Amazon to generate sales. But what are the other B2C (Business to Customers) channels that I can leverage in order to sell more pieces? I thought about distributors, but I knew unless I am able to create a 'Pull', no distributor or shopkeeper would entertain my product. Even if some shopkeepers or distributors agree to showcase my product, it will continue to gather dust because of a lack of awareness among buyers. I could try using other online channels such as Flipkart, Paytm Mall, Tata Cliq, etc. However, all these channels required getting a trademark for my brand. Since I was the manufacturer, I needed the brand registration or trademark in order to get listed on these platforms. Registering for a trademark would cost me approximately Rupees 10000. Moreover, if I list my product on these channels, I would have to again run the ad campaigns. Otherwise, the product would continue to languish at the bottom of the search results on these new platforms. With that in mind, I abandoned the idea of listing on Flipkart, Paytm Mall, Tata Cliq, etc.

Now, I shifted my focus on B2B (Business to Business) customers. Who are my B2B customers? How can I reach them? How can I position my product to these potential customers? These were some of the questions that took my time for the first week of July 2019. I made a comprehensive B2B strategy. That strategy included positioning my product as 'An exhaust fan that catches & kills mosquitoes', leveraging email campaigns and B2B platforms such as IndiaMart to reach out to B2B customers, and identifying real estate builders and architects/consultants as potential B2B customers.

From my previous real estate experience, I had the full database of real estate builders across India. Therefore, preparing a database of real estate developers and architects/consultants was straightforward. It didn't take any time whatsoever. I started using free email campaign services to send weekly email newsletters to my database of real estate developers & architects/consultants. At the same time, I had listed my product on IndiaMart. After 2 weeks of the campaign, I received 2 inquiries from real estate developers in Delhi NCR region. I visited these developers and showcased my product as well as submitted the quotation. The builders liked the product. They wanted at least 750 pieces. I said to myself, wow, B2B rocks. However, my joy was short-lived. One of the developers wanted a smaller size exhaust fan because he had already made a cut-out for installations in each & every apartment of the housing society. I visited that builder again and assured him that my team will do the necessary installation within the price quoted. However, that deal did not go through despite my full-fledged attempts. The other builder was rather casual, and there was no scope of him buying the exhaust fans from any of the vendors. However, that whole experience gave me the confidence that the product can be sold in the B2B market even if it takes time. In other words, I was now sure that both B2C and B2B are my customers. My strategy including the customers was well defined. I said to myself, it's just a matter of time before the product becomes a mainstream product. The month of July had passed by and I had no B2B customers. Few more sales had happened on Amazon. However, there were no extra reviews, neither good nor bad. I kept on focusing on my defined strategy. But sales volume did not increase even in the month of August 2019. I said to myself, alright, 2 more months of mosquito menace across India and surely the product will start selling well.

I was now getting impatient. There was hardly any improvement in sales on Amazon. 10-12 pieces a month. I did not have a lot of money to spend on ad campaigns. Whatever revenues I generated on Amazon went into the ad campaigns. B2B was not happening either despite working on it religiously as per the plan. I now decided to contact shopkeepers or distributors. But I knew if I just make a cold call or cold visit to these shopkeepers or distributors, they would simply turn me away saying 'Not interested'. I as well as my company would be looked down upon by these shopkeepers and distributors. So, I decided to visit shopkeepers or stores or distributors whom I knew through my references. Again, Sumit and Sunil provided me the contact details of 2 stores that they knew. I contacted both the stores. Both these stores were in Faridabad. The reference provided by Sumit did not respond. However, the reference provided by Sunil responded and we fixed up a meeting the next day.

I traveled to this store in NIT Faridabad. The person was warm and he looked at my product carefully. Again, I had already decided to position my product as 'an exhaust fan that also catches & kills mosquitoes'. Therefore, it was rather easy to explain the product to the store owner. He liked the product primarily because of additional features of mosquito catching and dual-LED besides the quality. He did compare my product with existing exhaust fans in the market such as by Havells, Usha, etc. Most of them were selling in the range of Rs 1200 to 1300. Therefore, he asked me to sell my product to him at a price of Rs 1000 inclusive of taxes. That was not at all possible for me. Even if I manufacture at a large scale, I won't be able to sell the product to these distributors at a price of Rs 1000 inclusive of taxes. His reasoning was that by pricing the product at Rs 1000 inclusive of taxes to him, he would be able to sell the product at Rs 1200, thereby making a profit of Rs 200. In other words, he wanted something that's comparable to existing brands such as Havells, Usha. I explained to him that my product is completely different. You can't compare an apple with an orange. He understood my point of view, but he countered that yours is a new product. You can start at a low price and gradually raise the price. I said I can definitely sell the product to you at Rs 1200 inclusive of taxes and then you can sell at Rs 1400 per piece. Well, we could not converge on pricing. I came back home thinking I would follow up with him and hopefully there is a middle ground.

The next day, I called the second store owner again. This time he responded to me. He was away for some days and therefore could not take my calls earlier. His store was in NIT Faridabad as well. He asked me to meet him on Friday at his store. I again traveled to NIT Faridabad. This store owner also liked the product. He was impressed with the quality. He did not set any price restrictions. I explained all the product features to him. Then we settled down to discuss the price. I gave him a price of Rs 1300 inclusive of taxes and the retail price of Rs 1650. In other words, he would be making a profit of Rs

350 on each sale. He was OK with that. We concluded our meeting with the commitment of delivering 10 pieces to him on the coming Sunday. I was delighted. I thought, wow, this distributor network has got going. If this store owner is able to sell the 10 pieces in the coming weeks, then, there it is. I would have successfully developed a distribution channel. A distributor channel that would keep giving me orders on a regular basis. And based on the confidence and terms generated with this store owner, I can contact many other store owners in different cities. It was a great success. I was truly delighted.

Coming Sunday, I traveled to this store owner and handed over 10 pieces to him. As part of our discussion, I did not make the bill yet. The idea was that this store owner would first sell these 10 pieces and then based on the performance or feedback from customers, I would bill him along with the next batch of pieces. I had accepted this term partly because I knew the store owner personally and partly because of the newness of my product. After handing over the 10 pieces to the store owner, we talked for a while. The store owner asked me if I had contacted other stores in Faridabad? I replied, yes, I did contact one more store but talks with that store had not moved forward. Basically, he was looking to become a wholesaler for my product in the entire Faridabad region. I couldn't be happier, that's what I wanted. Someone who takes my product and promotes rigorously. I replied, if you want to be the wholesaler of my product, then, I promise you I am not going to talk to any other store owner in Faridabad. But you have to put in a lot of effort to generate sales. He assured me that he will manage that. With that confidence, I came back home thinking, 'yes, phew, it's happening'.

It was already the second week of September 2019. After about a week's efforts on developing a network of distributors, results were showing. The distributor channel was happening. I was hoping for good things ahead. 10 days had passed by and I did not hear anything from the store owner. I called him to inquire about the status of sales or feedback on my product. He replied, 'oh, Shradh has started and therefore people are not buying new things'. Therefore, post-Shradh, I will definitely give you good news. I realized, oh gosh, 2 weeks would go by without any sales in 'Shradh'. But I was hopeful that come Navratri, the product would sell and maybe the store owner would be able to develop some retail outlets by that time. Since the store owner wanted to be the wholesaler of my product, therefore, he would develop retail outlets in Faridabad. In other words, he won't be indulging in retail sales himself, but instead, he will develop a chain of retail outlets and those retailers would sell to the end-customer. I was dreaming, I was dreaming what if this store owner is able to develop 20-25 retailers and each retailer sells 15-20 pieces a month, then, there it is. I would be easily selling 500 pieces a month. Wow, that sounds like an awesome plan. I guess that was the problem with me 'thinking way too ahead'. But I guess that's the case with every entrepreneur? No?

Well, the 'Shradh' period was over. It was the first day of Navratri. I did not call the store owner on the first day itself. I gave him time and instead called him on the 4th day of Navratri. However, the response was the same. No sales and no retailers. The store owner, though, had started talks with 2 retailers and those talks were positive. I asked him, why didn't he sell the product on his store itself? To which he replied, this is a Diwali season, and people are more interested in 'Diwali Lights'. I was now pulling hair from my receding hairline. That's another story and I can write one full book as to how I revived my hair organically. Maybe I can make a video. Anyways, thinking about my conversation with the store owner, I said to myself, firstly it was the Shradh period, then Diwali period, when the hell will this right time come for my product to sell? I was now remembering my own words about the 'Pull'. I realized without creating the necessary 'Pull', it would be difficult to sell through these distributors or store owners. But how do I create the 'Pull'? I knew in order to create the 'Pull', I needed to focus on 'Above The Line' or ATL advertising campaigns such as print media, radio, or banners. And all of that will cost me a huge amount of money. And I had no cash whatsoever to spend on those activities. Therefore, I simply decided to persist and stay patient with this store owner. Meanwhile, I continued to sell 10-12 pieces a month on Amazon. I also contacted some other store owners in Noida and Gurgaon, but all of it in vain. Again, without 'Pull', these distributors or store owners won't show any interest in my product.

I thought long and hard about creating the 'Pull' for my product within my own constraints. I made a comprehensive plan of leveraging content marketing to create a 'Pull' for my product. Content marketing included video marketing, Questions and Answers sites, social platforms, blogs. With those ideas, I got going into content marketing. I made 5-6 videos using free online video editing tools. I also started to answer 2-3 questions a day on Quora including on the problem of mosquitoes in India. I also wrote 2 articles a week. All of these activities gave me views, not a massive amount of views, but some views. However, it did not improve sales. Sales were still happening in a trickle. However, I decided to continue my work on content marketing despite no sales. Maybe after 1 year, things will change. That was my line of thinking. "Keep doing what you can do, and keep thinking of new ways to generate eyeballs as well as sales" was my mantra.

With sales not improving, I decided to change the product category on Amazon from 'Gardens & outdoors' to 'Home & Kitchen'. However, this change took its time. Moreover, with that change, I was no longer able to run Amazon sponsored campaigns. That was a bad thing as my sales stopped altogether for a good 10 days. After a gap of 10 days, my Amazon sponsored ads started to show again and sales returned. That was a big relief. Truly! Some sales are better than no sales. With all the marketing efforts, and after making some changes, sales grew partially to 25 pieces in the month of mid-October to mid-November. I thought, maybe that's how things are going to be for another 2-3 months. I was hoping that come March 2020 and I shall be selling at least 500 pieces a month. That was an ambitious target. With that target in mind, I decided to utilize print advertisements as well. I hired a local magazine company and placed my product advertisement for some micro-markets of the Delhi NCR region. Showcasing the ad for the whole of Delhi NCR region would have cost me a fortune. Therefore, I decided to just focus on 4 micro-markets namely Vasant Kunj, Sarita Vihar, and 2 sectors in Noida. The idea behind choosing these 4 micro-markets was that I would be able to reach out to not only the residents but also the store owners/shopkeepers. All of my marketing efforts were now geared towards creating the necessary 'Pull'.

Meanwhile, the 'Garg' of the Job working company called me. 'Sir Jee', where have you disappeared? I said, no no, I am here only, just trying hard to sell the product. Garg replied, yea, selling takes time, but your molds are sitting idle here at my facility, what shall I do with them? I said, let the molds remain there and I would soon send the raw material in order to start making the front cover pieces. Garg retorted, make sure that you do it soon, else, I will start charging you the monthly rent of Rs 1500 for keeping the molds at my facility. I said, 'Garg Jee', don't be this harsh on me. I am trying hard to sell the product and then I will start manufacturing on a monthly basis. Garg replied, Sir Jee, this is the norm in the industry, either start giving us orders or pay the rent for using our space. From my 'marketing' focus, I was brought down to 'this is the manufacturing industry in India' focus by Garg's words. I knew I had to take a call on manufacturing front cover pieces sooner than later. I had 380 pieces of front cover. Of which about 100 were sold. So, I still had plenty of them. But I was now calculating the cost of making another 1000 pieces of front cover. With a slight improvement in sales, I decided to manufacture 1000 pieces of front cover. I knew the front cover mold will take time to finetune and therefore if I start manufacturing the pieces now, maybe 1 month down the line, I will have 1000 pieces of front cover.

In the last week of November 2019, I sent the ABS raw material to Garg's facility in order to manufacture 1000 pieces of front cover. I visited Garg's facility in Mangolpuri and to my surprise as well as everyone's surprise, the front cover mold worked without any problem whatsoever. Garg started manufacturing 1000 pieces of front cover. And within 2 days, he sent the pieces to my place. Now, I had plenty of front cover pieces, but only a limited number of other parts. I knew I would be able to manufacture and procure all other parts in quick time except the 2 items namely the fan, and LED. These 2 items would have to come from China and it can take 1 month. I was now feeling confident that beginning March 2020, I would be able to sell 2000 pieces of my product on a monthly basis. That would be some achievement. However, it was possible. And even if demand increases, I would be able to deliver 5000 pieces a month as well with the existing supply chain. Manufacturing 5000 pieces a month will mean employing 10 workers for assembling and a supervisor to look after the operations as well as quality. I was confident that with the kind of supply chain I had developed, I would be able to deliver 5000 pieces a month. I would manufacture front cover and back cover pieces at Garg's facility and would source all the parts from India except fan and LED light. Fan and LED would have to be sourced from China. I started to think, what if I start to manufacture even fans in India? That thought just occurred to me. However, I knew, for that to happen, I would have to set-up a big plant. If not big, certainly a medium-size plant. My thoughts were running wild. I had ideas to manufacture other products as well. Products such as washing machines, ceiling fans, air purifiers. Of course, all these products would be different from the existing brands in the marketplace. I knew that I can't do it alone. I needed investors to back me. And based on my current sales, no investor would back me. I needed to touch 2000 sales a month with the Mosquiter product first.

Chapter 7

Scaling up

However, I started talking to investors. I talked to Himanshu as well as Sunil. Himanshu was occupied in his current project and therefore could not assess my plan. With Sunil, I discussed the plan to raise Rs 50 Lacs. I told Sunil, maybe you can gather 10 people over there in the UK and they would each invest Rs 5 Lacs. This way raising Rs 50 Lacs wouldn't be difficult. Sunil asked me about the detailed plan. I told him that Rs 50 Lacs would be spent on manufacturing as well as marketing 5000 pieces. And with proper marketing campaigns, selling 5000 pieces in 3-6 months would be possible. Sunil knew that I had already sold 100 pieces and therefore there is market acceptability of the product. There was a strong case to be made for the investment in my project. Sunil discussed this with a group of people in the UK, however, most people just talk about entrepreneurship and when it comes to real action, they prefer investing in property than backing startups. Sunil called me and explained to me the inclination of people with regard to investment. We both had a good laugh about it. Sunil, though, introduced me to a CA friend of his. I contacted that CA and we met the next day. I explained my product as well as the project to this CA. I even made a comprehensive business plan and submitted this plan to the CA. The CA would now take my plan to investors as well as debt providers including tapping some government-sponsored startup schemes. I knew all of this is going to take time.

Meanwhile, I also contacted one of my real estate customers. During my real estate business, I had helped this customer lease office space in Gurgaon. This customer is an angel investor and he had started an incubation center in the office space that he had leased in Gurgaon. Manoj, that angel investor, invited me to his office on a Saturday afternoon when he would have time to discuss my business plan. I reached his office at Sohna Road, Gurgaon. There were very few people on that day. I showed & explained my product to Manoj as well as gave a detailed business plan to him. At first, he was excited by the idea and the product itself. He was also excited about the fact that I had already sold 100 pieces. However, the issue with Manoj was that he had invested in or backed only internet Tech companies. He had no idea about the manufacturing domain other than the fact that it takes a hell of a lot of effort to crack a manufacturing business in India. Investing Rs 50 Lacs wasn't a big deal for him. He also knew that money would be recovered even if the company doesn't take off. He knew that by selling 5000 pieces money would be recovered. But he was still not excited about entering the manufacturing domain primarily because of valuation dynamics. He told me that most of the start-ups that he backs or invests in don't provide any profit even for a good 6-7 years. However, all these start-ups end up gaining a higher valuation on account of growth. I interrupted Manoj by saying, yea, all these Tech start-ups don't have a business model, rather a 'Robinhood' model. 'Robinhood' model? What's that? Manoj asked. I said, just like Robinhood used to steal money from the rich people and then subsequently distributed among poor people, likewise, all these Tech start-ups take money from rich investors and distribute among customers. To this, Manoj simply smiled. I wasn't sure if I had done the right thing by uttering these words.

In any case, he wasn't sure about an exit strategy from a manufacturing business. In a nutshell, he wasn't sure about the start-up ecosystem for a manufacturing company. To him, as far as manufacturing is concerned, India is simply a big market. A big market wherein multinationals such as Samsung, LG, Honda gain entry into the Indian market and set-up a plant to manufacture products and serve the Indian market. Ancillary units then evolve to supply parts to these multinationals. Top-Down manufacturing. To him, 'Make in India' is nothing but this. 'Make in India' only supports top-down manufacturing. There is no word or policy on start-up manufacturing or bottom-up manufacturing. Bottom-up manufacturing wherein an Indian entrepreneur starts with an idea in mind and over a period of time builds a sustainable large manufacturing business serving Indian as well as global customers. In his own experience, he had not seen such a manufacturing company from India. I concurred with him and I knew that it is going to be extremely difficult to find investors backing an Indian manufacturing start-up.

Manoj also highlighted that within the internet Tech space there are foreign investors who end up acquiring stake and therefore there is a high possibility for an Indian investor to exit with good returns. However, he wasn't sure about such a scenario in the Indian manufacturing space. Moreover, he knew that most of the Indian manufacturing companies as well as multinationals source a large volume of goods from China and simply sell in India. He highlighted the case of air-purifiers. Almost all air-purifiers are sourced from China and sold in India. All these Fast Moving Electrical Goods (FMEG) Indian companies simply indulge in contract manufacturing in China and then sell the finished products in India. In other words, Manoj wasn't confident in manufacturing in India itself. He highlighted the challenges of land, labor, cost of financing, and the effort required to obtain various approvals to start a manufacturing business in India. In other words, he did not want to enter a domain wherein there would be plenty of business-government interface. He was happy being in internet Tech space wherein there is virtually no business-government interface. Although he highlighted the lack of foresightedness among our policymakers when it came to internet Tech businesses as well.

He highlighted how most of the Indian internet tech companies are foreign-owned. Chinese and US companies have made India their digital colony. Google and Facebook take almost 80 - 85% of their advertisement revenues out from India. Flipkart, Ola, Zomato, Paytm are majority-owned by foreign investors, mainly Chinese and US investors. And the Indian government has not done anything on this front. Indian policymakers are simply happy being the market of over a billion people for foreign investors. The Indian policymakers simply don't even understand the difference between control and ownership, he said with a degree of frustration in his voice. I promptly asked him. How? What's the difference? He gave me an example of Facebook. Even though Facebook is majority-owned by foreign investors, but the control remains with the promoter 'Mark Zuckerberg'. In other words, even though he owns minority shares, but those shares are 'class A' shares thereby giving him the controlling power. Whereas in India, you saw what happened with Flipkart. Walmart bought it and stupid Indians were celebrating forgetting that almost 80% of the sales proceeds went to foreign investors with founders getting the remaining proceeds. In other words, profit was made by foreign investors. Of course, they would have paid some capital gain tax, but that's about it. India gained nothing. So, here are we with 2 foreign e-commerce giants in India, Amazon, and Walmart. So, who controls the online retail in India? You tell me, he asked with a degree of disdain in his voice towards our policymakers. The same is the case with other tech companies in India. Neither do they have the majority share nor do they have controlling power. The Indian government came up with a start-up India plan in January 2016, and the tax code was so horrible that the number of start-ups registered in India actually fell in the subsequent year. The start-up India plan was designed to invest or infuse Rs 10000 Crores in Indian start-ups over a period of 4 years and can you believe me only Rs 91 Crores have been infused 2 years into the program. In 2016, approximately 7500 startups were registered in India and after the launch of the start-up India campaign, in 2017, only 1300 start-ups were registered in India. Manoj was quoting from a trusted media source[1]. I was aghast to hear about such numbers. I wondered why then we as public and media keep celebrating the start-up India campaign? Why don't media bring these numbers in the public domain? I couldn't believe what I just heard from Manoj. He was dumbfounded as well and wondered why the government even tried to enter the start-up ecosystem? They could have left the start-up ecosystem to entrepreneurs and venture capital funds. All the government or policymakers could have done is just simplify the tax code and give Indian entrepreneurs the controlling power in their start-ups even though the very start-ups could be majority-owned by foreign investors.

---

[1] https://www.youtube.com/watch?v=V0zUcoVeyg0

Manoj even narrated the story of a manufacturing entrepreneur. That entrepreneur was going to make disposable crockery from biodegradable material obtained from tree leaves. The plastic disposable crockery is going to be discontinued soon and therefore this entrepreneur entered into manufacturing of biodegradable disposable crockery. He had access to funds. He partnered with some other people to get the land in Haridwar. Manoj stressed about the fact that see with access to funds and land, this entrepreneur still ended up in the maze of obtaining approvals. It took him almost 6-8 months to get so many approvals, fire safety, environmental protection, labor approval, building construction approval, building map approval, ESI & PF, etc. And trust me, nothing happened in a single-window system as has been proclaimed by various government authorities. This entrepreneur had to run pillar to pillar to obtain all these approvals and yes he did pay cash to officers to obtain faster approvals. Even with that, it took him almost 8 months. On top of that, he had bought 4 big CNC machines from China. And obtaining finance for these 4 machines from banks was a herculean task in itself. He had to provide land as collateral as well as some other personal guarantee. Moreover, the cost of financing is high. And now, his plant is undergoing installation & commissioning of these machines. In all probability, it is going to take another 6 months to start the operations. In other words, for someone with access to funds and land, it will take almost 1 and a half years to start the actual production work. And you are asking for funds for a manufacturing start-up? Very few investors would back a manufacturing start-up. I am not saying, 'No', but chances are very slim.

Listening to Manoj, I knew that he was hands-on with the start-up ecosystem in India. He wasn't particularly enthused with policymakers as well. But he had already made 5-6 investments in the Indian Tech start-ups. Therefore, he had no option but to go through the maze called the Indian start-up ecosystem. I knew he won't be investing in a manufacturing start-up, at least not in the foreseeable future. I even tried to persuade him with the recent announcement by the finance minister on dropping the tax rate to 15% for new manufacturing companies. Manoj wasn't enthused by this as well. He simply said, all of this has been done to bring in foreign money into India, which is not a bad step, but what are the other steps have they taken to simplify start-up manufacturing in India? Why are Indians going to China and bringing goods from there and simply selling in India? Now, he started to sound like me. I had similar questions in my mind when I started this manufacturing business. And during the course of my manufacturing journey, I understood the reasons for India's trade deficit with China. I knew that starting up was a challenge and now scaling up would be an even bigger challenge. Where would I get the money from? The government schemes or loans that support manufacturing companies simply do so against collateral or security. And I had no access to any collateral. Moreover, I wanted the investors' money not just for the money part but also for the mentorship part. I knew venture capital investors can guide the company in scaling up. I alone would find it a herculean task. We concluded our meeting with the possibility of talking again in the future.

I came home thinking about the scale-up. I knew customers are already querying me for a smaller size (6 inches blade) 'Mosquiter' machine. However, at this stage of my operations, all I have is this 8 inches blade machine. I knew making a 6 inches blade machine would mean repeating the processes that I executed to manufacture the 8 inches blade machine. And I knew fully well that mold making can drive me nuts. I knew I wouldn't have my own Tool-room to develop the molds for 6 inches blade machine. That would be too costly. I knew I didn't want to approach Daler or any other unorganized Tool-room operator to develop the molds for this 6 inches blade machine. The very thought of approaching Daler or any other unorganized Tool-room operator gave me the negative goosebumps. I almost felt that my heart would sink in if I try to develop the molds for this 6 inches blade machine in India. The mold making experience was so horrible that I didn't want to go through it again. So what are the options now? Keep quiet and focus on marketing and continue to sell this 8 inches 'Mosquiter' machine? Even for that, I needed money. And no investors would back me if I don't have a detailed business plan. A detailed business plan that not only comprises of the current product but also comprises of the future products. Manufacturing is all about adding new products, if not new products, then, various sizes of the same product in order to possess a complete catalog of the same product. And to make different sizes of the same product, I needed to develop molds, and that exercise is simply too painstaking. What should I do? I kept thinking for the coming days. There were 2 options. One, 'simply go through the pain of manufacturing in India' or 'go to China and develop the molds as well as the final product there and simply sell in India'. That's what many Fast Moving Electrical Goods (FMEG) companies do in India.

I knew by opting for option number 2, I would simply transfer the pain of setting up a manufacturing plant in India to Chinese manufacturers. In other words, I will have no worries. I will simply focus on brand building, marketing, and selling. However, if I choose option number 1, then, I would have to go through the maze of approvals, seek financing, and get access to funds. I was now seriously thinking why the hell did I end-up in manufacturing in the first place. Why did I even take a plunge? If starting up was a challenge, then, scaling up is a mountain. And why would any entrepreneur show to the world that he did it in India? He did it in the Indian manufacturing ecosystem. I mean, what's the fun about it? Why don't our government or policymakers make manufacturing friendly policies if they are serious about 'Make in India'? Why would someone take the pain of going through the maze of approvals? Why would someone borrow money at such high-interest rates? There is no economic sense to it. There is no economic sense to locking the high-interest rate money in land, machinery. The choice is between becoming a trader or manufacturer. And no wonder, most entrepreneurs choose to become traders in India. No wonder, our trade deficit with China is burgeoning year after year. No wonder, unemployment rates are high. No wonder, 'Make in India' is only about top-down manufacturing and not about bottom-up manufacturing.

My mind now started to shift positions. A position which many entrepreneurs in India take and that is to source goods from China and then sell in India. I also started thinking about taking my designs to China and develop the molds there. And then manufacture final products there and ship those finished products to India. I would simply focus on selling in the Indian marketplace. In other words, hire Chinese manufacturing companies as contract manufacturing companies and outsource the operations there.

India is a big market, that's what many Indian FMEG companies think as well. That's why they source manufactured goods from China and sell in India. India is a big market for foreign investors in Tech as well as in non-tech sectors. Set-up base in India, serve the Indian customers and take profits out of India. Well, at least, that's what advertising giants like Facebook and Google do. The Indian government, as well as policymakers, are happy or content with the idea of a 'marketplace of over 1 billion'. No wonder consumption continues to drive our economy. A nation's economy comprises of the following:

Economy = Consumption + Government Spending + Investment + Net Exports

And in the context of the Indian economy, consumption's proportion is approximately 60%.

Whereas in the context of the Chinese economy, consumption's proportion is approximately 40%.

This is precisely the reason we continue to hear from experts, economists alike about the need to increase the Investment's proportion in the Indian economy. And having gone through the maze of manufacturing in India, I would urge policymakers to invest big time in the manufacturing sector. I would urge policymakers to invest in bottom-up manufacturing. Let Indian start-up manufacturers make world-class competitive 'Made in India' products. Let us unleash the animal spirit among start-up manufacturing entrepreneurs. Focus on manufacturing is the need of the hour. Focus on bottom-up manufacturing is the need of the hour. And the success of the manufacturing sector can be judged by parameters or key performance indicators (KPIs).

Chapter 8

KPIs to judge the success or failure of 'Make in India' Program

I was now remembering the day when I completed the prototype. It was May 1, 2018. It had been 1 and a half years. Finally, the product was ready. I had started selling. I knew selling is going to be another beast altogether. If manufacturing was frustrating, then, selling will take its own time. However, selling was 100% in my hands. I wasn't dependent on anyone. In manufacturing, I was dependent on Daler to complete the mold on time. I was now thinking, had Daler completed the molds by February, then, maybe I would have gotten a good start by launching this product in the month of March 2019. But that was not to be. Thinking back about the manufacturing process, I started to structure all the issues that I had encountered. I also started to structure my thoughts with regards to scaling up. I also thought hard about getting investors on board to scale things up. I had promised Sumit to write about those issues. And I guess, it's time to address those issues. It's time to be blunt about those issues. It's time to bring those issues at the forefront and hopefully, policymakers would be able to look at these issues comprehensively and make the necessary changes in order to succeed in the 'Make in India' program.

But before I could gather any focus to start writing about these issues, I got a call from my manufacturing friend 'Bansal'.

What's up Sachin? Bansal asked.

I said, all fine Bansal Bhai, just thinking about the manufacturing sector and how it can be made simple for start-up entrepreneurs.

Bansal started laughing, and said, to hell with manufacturing issues, Bhai, don't waste time, now that your molds are ready and you have started selling, just keep on selling and don't divert your focus from it. There is no point in writing about the issues. No one will pay attention to whatever you write. I have been in the manufacturing sector for over a decade and nothing has changed for start-up entrepreneurs. Just GST has been put in place instead of the old taxing structure. Otherwise, process-wise, all else remains the same. Mold development used to take time in the past, and it still takes time. Scaling up used to be a challenge, and it still is a big challenge. So, don't waste any time whatsoever on writing or talking to people about manufacturing issues. Just get on with it and keep on selling. Anyways, I have organized a college get together this coming Sunday on 15th December 2019 in Gurgaon, and you must come. With that invitation, Bansal and I hung up the phone.

Coming Sunday, I reached Ambience Mall Gurgaon at 3 PM. Bansal was there. To my surprise, our packaging friend 'Rajesh' was there too. And there were 4 other common friends - Kalsi, Mitesh, Jolly, Dutta. Why did we meet at 3 PM? Well, it was wintertime, so starting early would mean we could leave early. Since most of them were married, so they would have to reach home on time, or else something bigger than manufacturing issues will pop up at home. Moreover, 3 PM is the time when most bars offer happy-hour packages. So, we could gulp more for the same price.

We ordered snacks and drinks.

Bansal patted my shoulder and said, 'you will succeed'.

He was in a very light mood. Rajesh was in a light mood as well. Well, they had been in the manufacturing business for over a decade, therefore, they had reached a stage wherein they were able to carry out their business on the phone itself. They had already done the hard yards and it was time to reap rewards by conducting business in a light-hearted way. However, my mind was still occupied with thoughts on the manufacturing sector, issues, scaling up. I wasn't worried, I was deep into the manufacturing sector. No no, I wasn't looking to transform the manufacturing sector. I knew my limitations. I was just thinking things should be simpler not just for me, of course, but for all other bottom-up manufacturing entrepreneurs.

Bansal had already gulped a Pint and was truly in a mood to make it a 'Patiala' evening. We all were talking about our college days. And most of them were getting nostalgic saying 'those were the best days'. Well, they didn't sing the 'summer of 69' song literally; but all of them were getting nostalgic. My mind too was now away from manufacturing. But all of a sudden, Kalsi raised the topics of politics and economy. Bansal and Rajesh resisted by saying, oh no, not again, don't start these WhatsApp university topics again. We have learned enough about politics, economy, religion on WhatsApp university. So, don't bring these topics again.
For a moment, there was silence. No one talked. But after that moment, people still ended up talking about politics, economy, etc. etc.

Everyone started to talk about the steps the ruling government must take to revive the economy. From the focus on rural economy to FDI to exports.

Bansal interjected, 'Nothing will take our economy forward if we don't focus on manufacturing'. Look, China and India were at the same point in 1980, and as things stand today, China is economically 4.5 times the size of India. China started to focus on manufacturing big time and is now a superpower. Bansal was speaking from his own manufacturing experience.

I nodded in agreement with Bansal. Yea, Bansal is right, only manufacturing can take the Indian economy forward. Focus on manufacturing will not only revive GDP growth but will also generate millions of jobs. Bansal was boldened by my support.

Bansal took out his iPhone. And showed India's trade deficit with China to everyone. Well, I did not focus on the trade deficit graph because I already knew it. I thought, wow, these guys have really made it. They all are carrying iPhones, and I am still into that early 2000s dumb phone. Bansal started speaking my language. I guess, anyone who is in manufacturing will speak this language.

Bansal highlighted the products we import from China and how these products can be easily made in India. But we don't make them in India because of a variety of reasons. Rajesh and I simply concurred with Bansal. Because we knew the limitations of Indian manufacturing.

Bansal proclaimed 'Manufacturing' in India can be considered successful if policymakers focus on 2 parameters.

I asked, what are those 2 parameters or KPIs. Well, I love the word 'KPI' a lot and therefore I insisted to use the word KPI instead of parameter.

Bansal said, first is the trade deficit with China - is it going down? Or going up? And second KPI is how much time does it take for an entrepreneur to fail in the manufacturing business in India?

Having been through the manufacturing start-up business, I concurred with Bansal and repeated those 2 KPIs again to drive home the point Bansal was making:

1. The trade deficit with China - Is it going down? Is it going up? We need to get that data.

2. How much time does it take for an entrepreneur to fail in the manufacturing business in India?

Bansal started assessing each of the KPIs one by one:

- The trade deficit with China:

Bansal took out his phone again and showed the trade deficit graph again to each and every one.

India Imports from China (US $ Billion), India Exports to China (US $ Billion) and Trade Deficit (US $ Billion)

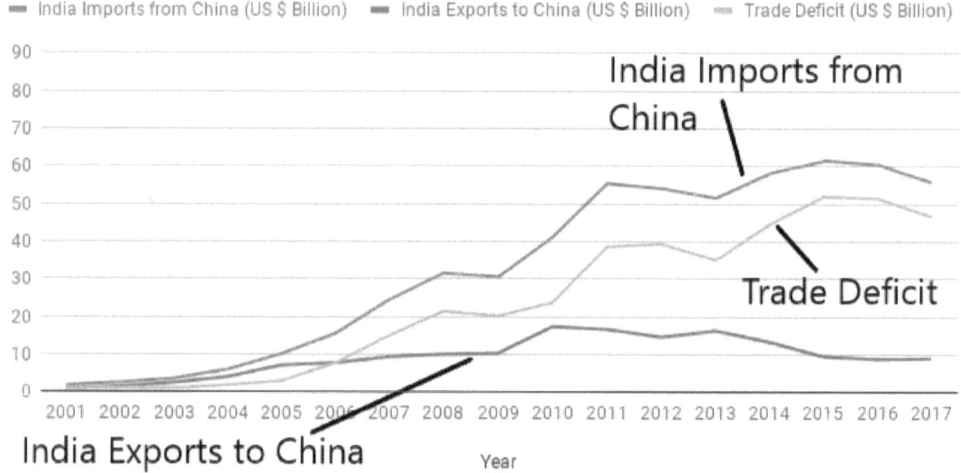

Source: 'PHD Research Bureau; Compiled from Trade Map Database'

He said, as can be seen from this graph that India's exports to China have not kept pace with India's imports from China. As a result, the trade deficit with China has followed a pattern similar to what India imports from China. This is worrisome. Why is this worrisome, he asked all of us? We remained silent. Bansal continued, this is worrisome because of the following reasons:

a. India's top imports from China

Let's have a look at what India imports from China. Bansal further showed the top ten import items to all of us:

1. Electrical machinery and equipment and parts thereof; sound recorders and reproducers, television.

2. Machinery, mechanical appliances, nuclear reactors, boilers; parts thereof

3. Organic chemicals

4. Plastics and articles thereof

5. Ships, boats and floating structures

6. Iron and steel

7. Fertilizers

8. Optical, photographic, cinematographic, measuring, checking, precision, medical or surgical

9. Articles of iron or steel

10. Vehicles other than railway or tramway rolling stock, and parts and accessories thereof

We just gave a cursory glance to the top ten imports from China.

Bansal said, barring 1 or 2 items, most items that India imports from China are all manufactured goods. The question that needs to be asked is 'when China can manufacture all these goods, what stops India from manufacturing these goods'? Wages are certainly not higher in India than in China. Then, what explains this trade deficit with China?

We asked Bansal, you should tell.

He said, yea, I will, but first let me show you guys India's top exports to China.

b. India's top exports to China

Let's now have a look at what India exports to China. Here are the top ten export items:

1. Cotton

2. Ores, slag and ash

3. Organic chemicals

4. Mineral fuels, mineral oils, and products of their distillation; bituminous substances

5. Copper and articles thereof

6. Salt; sulfur; earth and stone; plastering materials, lime, and cement

7. Machinery, mechanical appliances, nuclear reactors, boilers; parts thereof

8. Electrical machinery and equipment and parts thereof; sound recorders and reproducers, television

9. Animal or vegetable fats and oils and their cleavage products; prepared edible fats; animal

10. Plastics and articles thereof

He continued, barring 1 or 2 items, most items that India exports to China are all raw materials. China imports raw material from various countries including India and then exports manufactured goods to various countries including India. China has become the world's factory and India has lagged behind. There was no surprise in the data. Most of us had thought the same, but data further corroborated our line of thinking.

Bansal didn't stop at the data. He continued, what were successive Indian governments and policymakers doing to bring down the trade deficit with China? We as a nation shall certainly be asking this relevant question to our policymakers. Just imagine, if India were to neutralize trade deficit with China, this alone would create manufacturing goods worth 50 - 60 Billion US $ (approximately, 4 Lacs Crores Rupees) in India on a yearly basis. How many jobs would it create? We can't estimate that, but certainly, that number would be massive and probably close to 1 Crore manufacturing jobs. In other words, if India were to become a true manufacturing hub, then, consumption of those manufactured goods within India alone can create 1 Crore jobs. And it is highly likely that Indian entrepreneurs after conquering the Indian market will expand to overseas markets much like Chinese entrepreneurs. The overseas competition can further result in great products, new innovative products, and many more millions of jobs to people in India.

I thought, gosh, that's a good assessment by Bansal.

Bansal then shifted his focus on the second parameter or KPI.

- How much time does it take for an entrepreneur to fail in the manufacturing business in India?

There is no formal data on this. Of course, there can't be any formal data on this. How can we expect our policymakers to prepare a formal database on this question when they haven't done anything to address the India-China trade deficit? We are asking for too much from our policymakers.

For this parameter, Bansal said, I have to rely on my own experience. When I started the manufacturing business, It took me a good 1 year to get the mold ready and then start manufacturing the final pieces for a Chair. Well, Bansal is in the Chair manufacturing business.

I interjected, Bansal is right, it took me 8 months to get the molds ready.

Bansal said I can give countless examples of entrepreneurs who would concur that mold making or Die making and then manufacturing the final pieces in India takes a hell of a lot of time.

Bansal looked at me and said, Sachin Bhai you were lucky that you could complete your tasks in 8 months. Normally, it takes more than 8 months. Bansal continued, I am telling you, I as well as many other entrepreneurs would vouch that it takes just about 1 month to 45 days in China to get a high-quality mold ready. Therefore, from next time onwards, I am going to develop my new sets of molds in China. I don't want to waste my time in India.

So, if I had an idea and I wanted to try it in India. It would take 9-12 months to manufacture it. If that product does not succeed in the market, then, what would it mean? It would mean, I got my failure certificate in 1 year. whereas, the same failure certificate can be achieved in 2-3 months' time in China. Now, on the surface, it may not seem huge. But it is massive.

- It can break down any upcoming entrepreneur.

- It can stop innovation. People would shy away from trying new products. They would just bring tried and tested products.
- It can discourage people who are in safe & secure jobs but they still dream of becoming an entrepreneur. They also have an idea, but they don't try, because it takes a hell of a lot of time in India to try an idea. They don't have 1 year to fail. They could have tried if it took them 2-3 months to fail. But 1 year, forget about it.

I was speechless to hear Bansal's words. Everyone nodded in agreement, yea, time is critical.

In fact, Rajesh who was not as charged up as Bansal, said, True, Time is money. Bansal was unstoppable. Having highlighted the parameters or KPIs to judge the success or failure of the manufacturing sector in India, he started moving forward to identify the reasons for the negative performance of the chosen KPIs.

Chapter 9

Reasons for the lackluster performance of the manufacturing sector in India

Bansal elaborated, having spent more than a decade in the manufacturing sector in India, I can say with full certainty that there are 5 principal reasons for the lackluster performance of the manufacturing sector in India. Rajesh and I had already guessed those reasons in our minds. But Bansal listed the reasons.

1. Policymakers
2. Lack of organized Tool-rooms across India
3. Lack of common mechanism to obtain various approvals for scaling up the business
4. Lack of financial support
5. Lack of Skilled labor

Our common friends listed some other reasons such as culture, democracy, indiscipline. But Bansal stuck to his guns and said, the 5 reasons that I have listed are the principal reasons for negative performance on the KPIs that we just discussed resulting in the lackluster performance of the manufacturing sector in India.

We all were unanimous on policymakers. The bar had started to fill in. It was already 6 PM. My gosh, 3 hours simply flew. We were in no mood to pack-up either. I didn't drink that day. Bansal had also stopped after 2 pints. But others were enjoying the drinks and since we had met after such a long time, we stayed put for some more time.

Chapter 9.1

Reason Number 1 - Policy Makers

Bansal continued, yes, manufacturing or 'Make in India' can take off provided policymakers broaden their horizons by including startup entrepreneurs in the formal policymaking roles. Great policies are made by focusing on sector-specific details and this is where startup entrepreneurs can add value. However, unfortunately, India had lagged behind in this aspect. Whenever we read or come across a policy, all we see is a high-level idea or plan. However, there are no words on sector-specific details in that policy. And this is where the problem lies. Attention to sector-specific details is missing in these policy documents.

Jolly, who had lost his hair in rather quick time, said, what do you mean by policymakers? I keep hearing this word again and again but till today I have not understood the definition of policymakers. It sounds like a vague word to me. Who are the policymakers? Politicians? Bureaucrats? Politicians come and go and moreover, it is expecting way too much from a politician to understand the nuances of a diverse sector such as Manufacturing.

Bansal responded, yes Jolly, you are right. By policymakers, I mean, bureaucrats or Babus. The Babus stay in service for 3-4 decades and therefore they are the ones who make policies. All these Babus clear union civil services or state civil services exams and join at the age of 25-30 years with good intentions. However, since they haven't worked on the ground in respective sectors, therefore, they end up making high level plans without attention to details. And things do go wrong at the 'details' stage. Because this is where government-to-people interface comes up. And this is where we hear or read stories of malpractices or corruption.

Dutta nodded in agreement, yea, and then he started narrating his own experiences of dealing with government departments. He said, I applied for renewal of my passport and the experience was very nice. I logged onto the passport India website and provided my details and booked the appointment. Then, I traveled to the passport office which was managed by a private software company and everything was professional. Within 2 hours, the process was completed. The office too looked world-class. However, I also applied for a DL (driving license) recently and the experience was very bad. Based on my passport application experience, I had thought that applying for a driving license would be a smooth experience as well. Therefore, I took the appointment for the learner's license on the 'Sarathi' website. It was all nice till this time. However, when I reached the RTO office, firstly, the office resembled that old unhygienic Sarkari Daftar. The staff was unprofessional too. Applicants just came and sat on the computer for a minute and the process was completed. However, in my case, I took the tests, both written as well as the driving tests. And guess what, they failed me in the tests. My driving was not up to the standard according to their logic. However, I saw many people in their 50s getting the DL without any tests. Anyways, they asked me to take the appointment again by improving my driving skills. I said, what? My driving skills are good, and I can easily drive within any major city in India. However, they had already closed my case. I again took the appointment. I went to the RTO office again. And this time too, they failed me. I was speechless. I had wasted a good 3-4 days, and yet, I had not gotten the DL. I talked to people sitting outside the RTO office. And they all had a laugh. They were all agents. They asked me to give my papers to them. They told me that virtually all DL applications go through the agents. The Sarkari fee is nominal, however, the agents charged a fee of Rs 5000 (for learner's + permanent License). I understood this is a racket. And there is no way, I am going to clear these tests if I apply on my own. In other words, I had to go through that loop of agents. So, the point is, Passport service delivery has improved whereas DL service delivery is still corrupt. So, when Bansal talks about sector-specific details, I can very much understand that. Maybe they made a good high level plan for DL service, but at the details stage, things get messy resulting in malpractices or corruption.

Hearing these words, Mitesh too got going. Possible. But you can't paint the whole bureaucracy with the same brush. Bureaucracy basically comprises of 2 sets of people. One in policymaking role (higher level), and the other in the implementation role (details stage). The racket in the Driving License department that Dutta just talked about falls under the implementation side of the bureaucracy.

To which, Jolly replied, a common man can't distinguish between these fancy terms. All he/she wants is the delivery of service. When passport service can be good, why can't DL or building construction approvals service be good? Therefore, it becomes imperative for policymakers to pay attention to sector-specific details in great length and make policies that minimize malpractices.

Mitesh responded it takes time Jolly Bhai. Things are moving in the right direction. Technology is a great enabler. And bureaucracy is embracing the technology to resolve issues.

My gosh, hearing the word 'technology', Jolly got fired-up. What do you mean by technology? All these are fancy words or shall I say brainwashing words. Even if the policymaking side of bureaucracy embraces technology, then, at the implementation side, somebody has to press the button. Somebody has to click on 'OK'. And that's where rates are fixed. Dutta faced it in Driving License application and I had faced the same during the building construction approvals. Filing of form has moved online, however, think practically, somebody has to press the button to approve and that is where rates are fixed.

I added, yea, they shall privatize the implementation side of bureaucracy. This is happening in passport service, I guess, it can happen in other services as well.

Bansal though brought the focus back to manufacturing. He said, Bhai Mitesh, I don't know about technology, all I know is that manufacturing policy is lagging behind. Trust me, manufacturing is still the same. Barring the implementation of GST, there is no change in the last 10-12 years, at least for startup entrepreneurs. And I say this from experience. It seems to me that even the so-called policymaking side of bureaucracy has no clue about manufacturing.

Mitesh replied, how can you say that Babus are clueless about the manufacturing sector in India? Do you have any data? Do you know their current processes? Have you guys read the 'Make in India' document? I guess, No, but you start putting the onus on bureaucracy.

I responded, yes, I have read the 'Make in India' document and there is not a single word on 'Mold or Die' technologies or for that matter on 'Tool-room' technologies. Major initiatives under 'Make in India' are 'Invest India cell', 'Consolidated services and faster security clearances', 'Dedicated portal for business queries', 'Easing policies and laws', 'Interactions with users/visitors', 'The companies (Amendment) Act, 2015', 'An investor facilitation cell', 'Japan plus and Korea plus', 'Protecting minority investors'. These are all business-related processes, but what about processes related to manufacturing technologies? Mold-making technologies and Tool-room technologies are at the heart of any manufacturing. Even if you want to make a simple item like 'safety pin', you first need to develop the 'Die'. Similarly, the chair you are sitting on requires the development of 'Die'. Thereafter, final pieces are manufactured in the production line.

Bansal added I have spent more than a decade in the manufacturing sector. I know how difficult things are. Then, why shouldn't people like me be in the policymaking committee? Again, I say, it's not a question of intelligence, it's a question of knowing, experience. Take the example of this bar, now, you tell me, Mitesh, you are intelligent, but can you make policies for the restaurant sector? Do you know the details such as peak days, peak months, fixed costs, variable costs, starting-up? No, you don't know, and neither do bureaucrats know. Then, why aren't the restaurant owners involved in restaurant policies? Why aren't tourism operators involved in tourism policies?

Mitesh retorted, no no, you are wrong again Bansal Bhai, the respective ministry takes suggestions from entrepreneurs. I myself have provided feedback on e-gov portals on various topics.

Hearing that, 'Bansal' started laughing, haha, this is just for namesake. The real policies are made on the golf course or Delhi Gymkhana club. In any case, even if I accept your argument, then, why aren't we seeing results? Why is our trade deficit with China rising year after year? Manufacturing in India is still the same. I am talking about start-up manufacturing. It took me a good 5 years to stabilize in my work. Not many people will be willing to devote this much time. Mold making is a heartbreaking process. Scaling up is equally difficult. And by the time you think you have now stabilized, the traders start trading goods from China and we are back to square one. It's so tough.

I asked Mitesh when the so-called policymaking side of bureaucracy is talking about technology, then, why the hell aren't they talking about promoting Tool-room technology or mold making technology? Our Tool-rooms and mold-making processes are not only outdated, unorganized but also the capacity is too low. Why haven't they focused on that? It's not a small matter, it's a question of 60+ billion USD (4.2 Lacs Crores) on a yearly basis. After all, our trade deficit with China is 60+ billion USD.

To which, Bansal added, policymakers are oblivious of these terms Sachin Bhai. They don't know a damn thing about Tool-room, mold or die making, or for that matter scaling up a manufacturing business. Things are so tough.

I said, yea, I am terrified of developing new sets of molds. And at the same time, I am aware of the challenges that I will have to face for getting approvals for scaling up. Taking a dig at Mitesh, I further said, somebody from the so-called implementation side of bureaucracy would have to click the 'OK' button for granting approvals. And that can be a painstaking process.

Bansal too nodded in agreement with me. This is what has happened in India when it comes to the manufacturing sector. The medium and small scale enterprises are the bedrock of any economy. These enterprises not only bring innovative products to the market but also provide the bulk of employment. As per government own data, the manufacturing sector contributes about 16% to Indian GDP. The target is 25%. An increase in manufacturing sector output would not only boost demand but also provide millions of jobs. We have been hearing about the need for massive growth in the manufacturing sector, yet, government after government, the sector continues to languish. Why? Yes, you guessed it right. Attention to sector-specific details is missing.

Rajesh who was enjoying the evening until that point, added, that the 'Incredible India', 'Make in India', 'Startup India' programs are wonderful programs. But the question that arises is who is making policies for these wonderful programs? All these programs have wonderful websites, PowerPoint presentations, Logos, audio, video, etc. But what about the real content? The real content can and shall only be prepared by the real startup entrepreneurs as highlighted by Bansal. It's time to involve real startup entrepreneurs in policy-making for different sectors. Tourism entrepreneurs will make tourism policy. Manufacturing entrepreneurs will make 'Make in India' policy and so on. It's time people and media take up this issue vociferously.

Bansal said, yea, and he stressed the point that it's not a question of intelligence, rather it's a question of experience. A start-up entrepreneur certainly knows the missing links better than any Babu.

Mitesh was still not convinced.

Kalsi guessed it and said maybe Mitesh you are not convinced because maybe someone in your distant family is in bureaucracy?

Mitesh said, no-no, but you all know that my father was in a government department, but he was in execution role, not in policymaking role. Policymaking happens at a higher level.

Bansal was in no mood to give up. He continued, 'Make in India' or manufacturing is a serious and well-intentioned program. However, the questions that arise are 'Are real people drafting that policy'? Are entrepreneurs involved in drafting that policy? Only a startup entrepreneur knows what's needed to rectify the issues plaguing the sector. An entrepreneur has devoted many years in understanding the sector, in understanding different processes, in understanding different steps. That's what is missing from the 'Make in India' program.

I repeated myself, yea, there is hardly any word on 'Tool-room' or 'molds' in the 'Make in India' policy. Since mold making had driven me crazy, I again stressed on the importance of Mold or Die. Be it 'textile manufacturing, auto manufacturing, electrical manufacturing, electronics manufacturing, toy manufacturing', all kinds of manufacturing require 'Mold' or Die'. Big companies with access to capital can develop their own Tool-rooms, but small entrepreneurs can't develop their own Tool-rooms. They rely on external vendors to develop the mold. And from my own journey, I can tell you guys, the external Tool-room operators are highly unorganized. These unorganized Tool-room operators end up developing inferior quality mold in a much longer time period. No wonder, the manufacturing sector continues to lag. No wonder, the trade deficit with China continues to soar.

To counter the argument that the 'manufacturing' sector is not languishing in India, Mitesh showed some numbers or media reports related to Samsung doubling the mobile phone manufacturing in India.

I said, Mitesh, this is what we call 'top-down manufacturing'. All these companies such as Maruti, Samsung have access to capital and therefore these companies are in a position to double or triple down production. But these companies don't create the bulk of the jobs. In fact, when you hear about terms like automation in manufacturing, it is to do with these companies. Since they have access to capital, they automate their production by deploying robots, high-tech machinery. It's sad that common people and media do fall prey to these numbers. People and media get carried away thinking that all is well with the manufacturing sector in India and things are moving up. However, people and media again forget to pose some tough questions. Questions like, 'if manufacturing is moving up, then, how the hell this trade deficit is rising with China?', 'Why aren't our entrepreneurs producing simple items like chappals, Diwali light, Holi Pichkari, toys in India?', 'Why are our entrepreneurs becoming traders and not indulging in real manufacturing of these simple items?', 'Why is that all the goods sold in markets such as in Chandni chowk, Bhagirathi palace are sourced from China?'. All these questions, tough questions, would act as an eyeopener.

Listening to my argument about top-down manufacturing, Bansal said, the problem lies in the lack of understanding about manufacturing among the Babus. By lack of understanding, I mean, they don't seem to understand the difference between top-down manufacturing and bottom-up manufacturing. Let me tell you the difference.

Top-down manufacturing means a large multi-national or a large national company comes and sets up a base in a particular city. This company may be producing cars, phones, air-conditioners, or washing machines, etc. As soon as this large company sets up base in a particular city, the manufacturing ecosystem evolves in that city. Take the case of Maruti, it started operations in Gurgaon, and subsequently, ancillary manufacturing units supplying different parts such as nuts/bolts, clutches, brake system, gear system, piston, flywheel came up in Gurgaon. All these ancillary manufacturing companies were principal suppliers to Maruti. However, over time, as other car manufacturers came to Gurgaon, the ancillary manufacturers expanded their output to supply to new car manufacturers. This whole evolution of manufacturing is known as top-down manufacturing. India has done well in this aspect because of the size of the Indian market. A big company looks at the demand and the size of the Indian market and then decides to set up base. Most of the automation happens in this kind of manufacturing. This is also known as capital intensive manufacturing.

Whereas bottom-up manufacturing means the evolution of a product idea in an entrepreneur's mind and then manufacturing it. This idea could be about manufacturing any products such as toys, agarbatti, chappals, new innovative products, etc. A big company such as Maruti, Samsung, LG won't be producing these items. Only an entrepreneur with an idea can take the plunge and manufacture these products. However, an Indian entrepreneur chooses to go to China and buy these everyday household goods from China and then sell in India. In other words, there is no focus on bottom-up manufacturing in India. There is no policy to encourage bottom-up manufacturing in India. Noone at the policy level is asking these questions. Questions such as 'why is an Indian entrepreneur going to China?', 'what can be done that encourages the manufacturing of everyday household goods in India?'. These are the sorts of questions policymakers shall be asking to themselves in order to boost bottom-up manufacturing in India. This kind of manufacturing is also known as labor-intensive manufacturing. This is where the bulk of manufacturing jobs are created. But since India is importing most of these simple household goods from China, therefore, jobs are being created in China and not in India.

Therefore, it becomes paramount for Prime minister or minister in charge to look at this issue holistically, Rajesh said. If this problem is studied and analyzed holistically, then, surely the manufacturing policymaking committee will have a different look. This committee will comprise of people who understand manufacturing in-and-out. This committee will include people who will have an understanding related to processes, land, financing, sourcing, environment, and skill development.

Mitesh was not convinced, so all you intelligent folks, how shall a policy drafting committee look like?

I said, Mitesh, it's not a question of intelligence, it's a question of knowing, the question of experience. Why don't you get this?

Bansal though started explaining the structure of a policymaking committee. A policy-making committee shall be a diverse committee. This committee shall include 5-6 startup entrepreneurs, 5-6 big industrialists, environmentalists, 2-3 financial experts. This committee shall be a formal committee. Startup entrepreneurs shall not be restricted only to give their feedback online on that e-gov portal. They shall be part of the formal policymaking committee. Startup entrepreneurs, industrialists, environmentalists, and financial experts shall brainstorm hard for weeks to formulate a policy that encourages innovation, startups, competition, and inclusive growth. Take the case of tech businesses. The tech sector has grown in India. From Information Technology services in the 1990s and early 2000s to digitalization in 2010s, the tech businesses have flourished in India. The success of Tech businesses is because of the absence of Babus from this sector.

Bansal continued, the need of the hour is to leave the sectors to its entrepreneurs. Information Technology sector was left to its entrepreneurs and they really created a fabulous sector generating jobs as well as value for shareholders. The policy-making committee can be chosen by the minister in charge by using a well defined transparent process. The members of this committee shall be rotated or changed after a specific time period. Startup entrepreneurs shall be encouraged to list down the missing links in the success of that particular sector. The wisdom of industrialists in the committee can be leveraged to scale up the entire sector. The policy can then be put online and left open to ideas from other entrepreneurs in the sector. The policy-making committee can be given a deadline to formalize the policy. Economies are driven by entrepreneurs.

Why am I not involved in the process of making a 'manufacturing policy' in India? Why is 'Sachin' not involved in making the manufacturing policy in India? Why are other such entrepreneurs oblivious of the manufacturing policy? Why isn't Indian state learning from the success of India's Information Technology sector? Why is the Indian state not leaving the work of entrepreneurs to entrepreneurs? Why do they keep interfering in entrepreneurship? Where is the concept of 'minimum government and maximum governance'?

Rajesh then touched upon GST. He said, look how badly this GST has been implemented.

To which, Mitesh replied, you mean multiple tax rates? Before Rajesh could say anything, Mitesh asked, tell me, do you want to levy the same tax rate on a 'Hawai Chappal' and a 'Mercedes car'? I mean, you guys have no idea and are simply barking like street dogs.

Mitesh continued, no tax structure, as well as a technology solution, can be implemented without any glitches. It takes time. It's just been 2+ years since GST was implemented and in a matter of a year or two, things will settle down.

Rajesh did not respond. In fact, I took this up and I said, Mitesh, you would agree that most commentators including government ministers, Babus, experts, economists, industrialists were of the view that post-GST, the GDP growth rate would increase by 1.5 to 2 percentage points. Right?

Mitesh replied in affirmative, yea, but that was just to sell the idea to everyone including the public.

I said, true, it's been almost 2 years since GST (GST was implemented on 1 July 2017), and did the GDP growth rate increase by 1.5 to 2 percentage points as was claimed by all commentators?

Mitesh replied in negative, of course not, the GDP growth rate is falling as per government data. And it's about 5% in December 2019. I say it again, it was done to sell the idea so that GST can be implemented.

Rajesh said, OK, Agreed, but I ask you, why didn't the GDP growth increase post-GST?

Mitesh, no idea, I say it again, maybe that was their selling point to implement the GST.

I said, No, GST is a wonderful idea but it has been implemented badly.

Mitesh, How?

I said I had talked to various traders in Chandni Chowk, Meerut, Noida and they all are scared.

Mitesh: Scared? Why?

I said, let's take an example of a trader in Chandni Chowk. This trader was doing his business mostly in cash. Why?

Mitesh said, you tell, maybe to save on income tax?

I said, yea, before GST, this trader was doing his business in cash to save on income tax. Let us suppose he was doing a yearly business of Rs 1 Crore. But he would show the yearly business of Rs 30-35 Lacs on the book. He would do so to save on income tax.

Mitesh nodded in agreement. Understood, next?

I said, now that he was officially doing a yearly business of Rs 30-35 Lacs, how could he suddenly show Rs 1 Crore business? Wouldn't tax Babus reach his business place and ask for the historical records? If not all historical records, but, surely, the Tax Babus would ask for the last 5-10 years of transactions. Right?

Mitesh said, yea, that's absolutely right. But why does he need to show Rs 1 Crore business after GST?

I said, GST has a well-defined chain, wherein it is difficult to avoid the entire supply chain for any trader or business. Therefore, if you are a trader and you are buying material from various suppliers, then, it would be very difficult to hide from this entire supply chain. All these suppliers would definitely report their buyers and therefore the trader would become visible.

Mitesh said, agreed, so, what are these traders doing now post GST?

I replied they have reduced their business to Rs 35-40 Lacs. In other words, they are doing less business. They would do Rs 35-40 Lacs worth of business in the first year, Rs 50-60 Lacs worth of business in the second year, Rs 75-85 Lacs worth of business in the third year, and Rs 1-1.2 Crore worth of business in 4th year. Therefore, they would reach their pre GST levels of business in the 3rd or 4th year after the implementation of GST.

Mitesh said, I understand, what are the negatives of such a move?

I said, many, firstly, India is a big country. There are 4 to 5 Crores traders, they all would do less business in the first 3-4 years. What it means is that they would cut down on people that they used to employ. Trading was mostly an informal sector, therefore, unemployment would increase in the informal sector because of GST.

Mitesh asked, but didn't demonetization increase the unemployment in the informal sector?

I replied, yea, it did, but that was temporary, increase in unemployment in informal sector post-GST is very large. Just think of a trader who would employ 2 helpers to do Rs 1 Crore business would now employ just 1 helper to do Rs 30-35 Lacs worth of business.

Mitesh said, yea, right. What are the other negatives?

I replied, inflation, inflation would increase, if not, to an alarming extent, but certainly it will increase. Because the goods entering the market from the informal sector have reduced. Now only the formal sector is supplying those goods. If the informal sector was also supplying the pre GST levels of Goods in the market, then, inflation would have dropped down further.

Mitesh said, yea.

I continued, the other negative is the government in power will lose the support of the trading community. If not in high numbers, then, surely, they would lose some support.

Mitesh said, then, what could have the government done to rectify this error?

I replied, they could have added a clause in the Constitutional amendment act that small traders or small businesses would not be subjected to past business transactions scrutiny. They could have given this confidence to traders and businesses. After all, the economy is done on confidence. And when traders or businesses are scared, how the hell do you expect the GDP to increase by 1.5 to 2 percentage points?

Mitesh said, good point, but why didn't the government think of this? Why didn't the government added this clause in the constitution amendment act?

I replied, again, the lack of attention to 'details'. They should have really involved small traders or small businesses in the GST policymaking process.

Mitesh replied, not correct, the ruling government couldn't bring in the clause on past business transactions in the GST amendment act because of pressure from other political parties. Had the ruling government done so, then, other political parties would have labeled the government as 'suit-boot kee sarkar'. Therefore, the ruling government did not want to be seen as 'suit-boot kee sarkar'. Babus were not responsible, it's our political system. Why don't you guys get this point? We are largely a socialist or welfare country. Take money from rich and middle-class and then distribute among the poor.

Bansal and I nodded in agreement with Mitesh. But, we still persisted, that, policies are made and implemented without paying attention to sector-specific details.

Mitesh, no, an overview or final goal is given to Babus by the minister-in-charge, and then, the Babus make and implement the policies. And since most politicians want reelection, therefore, the goal is to help the poor. Because that's where the bulk of the votes are. However, I am willing to concede that in the framing and implementation of these policies, some malpractices may be adopted.

I said, no no, malpractices occur because not enough attention to 'details' is paid while making the policies.

Bansal too added, and this can be overcome by involving sector-specific entrepreneurs in the formal roles in the policymaking process.

Mitesh said that would almost mean changing the Indian governance system. I don't think it's possible.

Bansal replied, so what? Why can't the Indian governance system be changed or upgraded? Don't forget, we have about 10000 or 15000 years of civilization. So, there were governance systems at all times. Why should we say that the governance system handed over by the British to us is the best? British knew that they couldn't govern India without the Babus. British named them 'Commissioner' and 'Collector', which is nothing but the names given to the middlemen.

I took up from where Bansal left and said, the Indian Information Technology sector has shown that India can be a success story when the sector is left to its entrepreneurs. I bet you, you start involving sector-specific entrepreneurs in the Indian ecosystem and every sector in the Indian ecosystem will flourish. We won't need best practices from world bank or IMF, we won't need to learn to manufacture from China, we won't need world bank recommendations on ease of doing business in India, we won't need any global benchmarks, we will simply do it.

With that deep and animated discussion, we ordered for dinner. It was already 10 PM. Post dinner, we all shared the bill and headed home. Even though we ended up discussing the WhatsApp university topics such as economy, politics, bureaucracy, we still had fun and decided to make these kinds of get-together a monthly or quarterly affair.

3 days later on 18th December 2019, I traveled to Bansal's plant. Well, I was visiting the Mangolpuri Industrial Area to meet the 'Garg' of the job working company. So, I also decided to make a visit to Bansal's plant as well. We talked about our businesses. Bansal was looking to hire a senior fellow for his operations so that he can focus on the strategic side of his business. He asked me if I knew someone with the right talent and skills. I said I will search for such a person in my network and come back to you.

Bansal also said I had asked you to not think or write about manufacturing issues. But now, I am telling you Sachin, you must write. No matter, if anyone reads or not, but you must write. After that last week's conversation in the bar, I thought hard for a week, and I am now convinced that we all shall strive for a solution. We all means, all stakeholders in the manufacturing sector including you and me. We should not leave the sector to Babus. Therefore, writing is important. Therefore, you must write. We will keep talking and based on our experiences, we will write. The manufacturing policy or 'Make in India' policy' shall not be left to Babus. We shall strive to become part of the policy. Startup entrepreneurs shall become part of the policymaking committee. Policies are made by people and if right 'people' are placed at the right roles, then, right policies can be achieved.

I said, all right, we will continue to meet on a weekly basis and keep discussing the issues plaguing the manufacturing sector in India. You and I already know those issues from our own experiences, therefore, we will just structure our thoughts and write.

Chapter 9.2

Reason Number 2 - Lack of Tool-rooms across India

Even though Bansal and I had promised to meet on a weekly basis, but we did not meet for the next 2-3 weeks. We got occupied in our work. That's the nature of entrepreneurs. Whatever the situation or policy is, they just get on with the job.

Bansal called me, Sachin, there is a machine tool expo in Greater Noida in the first week of January 2020. Daler and I are going to visit. Maybe this expo could be of interest to you as well. Why don't you come?

I said, Bhai, I don't think that these exhibitions will be of any use to me at this stage of my manufacturing career. But I will see.

Even though the expo center was just 10 minutes drive away from my home, I saw no purpose in visiting the expo. The same evening I was talking to Sumit and I told him about the event. Sumit got interested and said maybe we can visit in the second half.

I said, alright, we can go. We can have a look at different machines for different manufacturing purposes.

Sumit and I visited the expo center and Bansal was there too. Daler was accompanying Bansal. We greeted each other. The weather was nice and sunny. Therefore, it wasn't as cold as it was during the whole of December 2019. The exhibition center was large and clean. There was a proper arrangement for parking, refreshments. The restrooms were hygienic too. Unlike the Pragati Maidan exhibitions, wherein everything had become crowded including the parking places, bad restrooms. This exhibition in Greater Noida was a pleasant surprise for me. I said to myself, not bad.

We moved around the entire hall and saw various machines. Big CNC machines for different purposes such as milling, packaging, grinding, etc. Many suppliers from China, South Korea, Germany, Japan had set up the stalls. It was by no means an ordinary event. Daler was interested in polishing machines whereas Bansal was looking for a big injection molding machine that can produce 600 Grams of a piece rather easily. I was not interested in any machines. I was just there to see, and learn. Sumit was not going to buy any machines either, he was excited to see different machines as well.

We were just talking in the hall, visiting different stalls. Sumit then said I am also looking to develop a different kind of toy airplane.
Bansal was perplexed, a toy airplane? Why?
Sumit said, yea, my son was asking for a toy airplane. Then, I searched online. There were many options. However, most of them had a good design but cheap material. Moreover, the toy airplanes that I found were all running airplanes. In other words, there was not a single model that can fly.
I said, why don't you visit the Chandni Chowk market wherein you might get the product you are looking for.
Sumit replied in negative, no no, I did not find it online as well as in the Chandni Chowk market.
I said, so, you are looking for something really specific.

Sumit replied, yea.

I did not understand what he was looking for. But surely, he had a clear idea of what he was looking for.

Sumit then said I would have built it and made it a business if I was not in a 9 to 6 job. I understand the whole concept of developing such a toy airplane that can fly.

Bansal and I had a laugh.

Sumit asked, what happened? What was so funny about it?

Bansal said, Sumit Bhai, we laughed not because you have come up with an idea, but because we know how difficult it will be to develop such a thing. Therefore, Bansal said, Sumit Bhai, forget about it and instead keep the focus on your stable job.

Bansal and I knew that Sumit can not build it. Not because of the talent, but because of the time, it will take. We knew Sumit won't have 8-9 months to develop something and then sell it on a larger scale. He simply was fascinated with this idea of a toy airplane. A different kind of toy airplane. However, having spent considerable time in the manufacturing sector, we knew Sumit would not be able to take the step to develop it because it's gonna take a long time to first develop the mold, build the supply chain, then manufacture, assemble, and then sell it on a larger scale.

All this while, Daler was just focused on his search for polishing machines. We stopped at a Chinese stall and they had a massive polishing machine on display. It looked magnificent. Well, despite being a Mechanical Engineer, I looked at all the machines in that expo in awe and wonder. I was blown away by the design, the looks, the capacity, and the size of the machines on display in the entire expo. Daler talked for a bit with the sales representative and asked for the polishing machine's configurations as well as the landing price in Delhi. He also enquired about the various financing plans. Having gathered all the info, Daler then took the catalog of the company for future discussions. It appeared to me that the visit to the expo was beneficial to Daler. The rest of us were there just for learning's sake.

We then took a break from stall visits. We went outside the hall and found a coffee shop. Being an ISKCON devotee, Sumit did not take anything. We all ordered a Tea.

Bansal then got going and said to Sumit, Bhai, having an idea is one thing but executing it is another thing. I am not discouraging you, I am just stating the facts. Who knows your toy airplane idea may click or may not click. But building it in the first place is a herculean task in itself. Sachin knows it, he is going through that journey. And I am sure you are aware of his journey as well.

Sumit nodded in agreement, yea, you are right. I keep talking to Sachin on a daily basis and I am aware of the challenges faced by a manufacturing startup entrepreneur. I am aware of the challenges he had to face in starting up and now in scaling up.

Bansal then looked at me and said, see, an idea of a different kind of toy airplane had been killed even without attempting to develop it. Why?

I said, yea, you are right Bansal. Sumit knows he simply can't spend 1 year on developing something which may or may not click.

Bansal replied the bottom line is Sumit won't attempt it. He won't attempt it because of the amount of time it would take to develop something like this. He would have taken the risk of developing it if the amount of time to develop it was less, say 2-3 months. Maybe he would have gotten the energy for 2-3 months to build it and then see if it can click or not in the marketplace.

Sumit said, possible. But surely, 1 year is too long a time period for someone like me who is settled in a well-established job.

I nodded in agreement, yea, there would be millions of such Sumits across India with ideas. But they don't have 1 year to spend on working on their ideas. Why can't this time period of developing something be reduced from 1 year to 2-3 months?

Bansal said It can be done. It certainly can be, provided we as a nation focus on creating Tool-rooms across India. Not just a few Tool-rooms, but Tool-room capitals across states in India. I mean, at a policy level. Few entrepreneurs setting-up Tool-rooms won't serve the purpose. It has to be done at a policy level. Large Industrialists and enterprises develop their own Tool-rooms (top-down manufacturing), but, a start-up entrepreneur or someone with an idea has no money to develop his or her Tool-room (bottom-up manufacturing). It's too costly. Therefore, he or she ends up visiting the scattered and unorganized Tool-rooms (or workshops) to develop the mold or die. And all these entrepreneurs go through the cycle that You and I went through. Bansal didn't mind calling Daler's Tool-room as an unorganized Tool-room even though Daler was present there. Bansal and Daler had known each other for a good 9-10 years. Daler was listening patiently. He was at ease and chilled out.

Bansal continued, an unorganized Tool-room (workshop) operator would promise a delivery in 2-3 months only to disappoint the entrepreneur. The real-time taken is close to 8-9 months unless one is developing a simple mold for mugs and buckets. Most entrepreneurs would back out from taking the plunge. Some with deep pockets would go to China and get their mold ready in 1 month. Some like us would simply be left at the mercy of the unorganized Tool-room operators.

Sumit asked, but all these kinds of machine tool exhibitions happen every year in different parts of the country, surely, people are buying machines.

Bansal said, of course, people are buying machines. I also buy machines. Daler buys machines as well. But trust me, our capacity is too low. Daler has just 4 machines. He is considering buying another machine in the next 2-3 years. Therefore, he has started to look for machines. But this is minuscule. With this kind of capacity, Daler can't develop high-quality molds in a quick time period.

Daler just smiled, he also knew his own limitations. However, Daler added, Tool-room is at the heart of any manufacturing business. After all, high-quality Molds or Dies are developed in a Tool-room. Be it a textile manufacturing, auto manufacturing, electrical products manufacturing, toy manufacturing, consumer products manufacturing, all kinds of manufacturing require Mold or Die.

Bansal interjected, Sachin, you are reading 'Make in India' policy document. Did you come across or read about molds in 'Make in India' policy? Did you read about Tool-rooms in 'Make in India' policy?

I said, No!

Bansal said I knew it. Well, that policy was made by unreal people. The new 'Make in India' policy shall be made by real people. Real people who know what a Tool-room is and who know the importance of mold and Tool-room.

Bansal again brought out the list of import items from China. He again showed the top ten imports from China and he stressed, see, the majority of the import items are manufacturing items that require the development of Mold or Die. Pointing his finger at Daler, Bansal said, when China can develop mold in 1 month, what stops India to develop that mold in 2 months?

Daler replied we can certainly do that provided we get our policy right. Daler said, we have a democratic system and China has a one-party system, therefore, making policies over there is relatively easy.

My Gosh, I didn't expect Daler to be this intelligent.

Sumit said, yea, making a good policy here in India is difficult.

However, Bansal said, it's not that difficult. Startup entrepreneurs shall be involved in the policymaking committee. There are 28 states and 9 union territories across India.

Let's focus on the 28 states first. Each state has a population larger than many countries in the world. Why can't each state has its own Tool-room capital? Haryana can have its own Tool-room capital, Uttar Pradesh can have 2 Tool-rooms capitals, and so on.

I said, true, I thought for a while and further added, however, these Tool-rooms capitals would require state support. Land, skilled labor, credit. These are the 3 ingredients to make Tool-rooms capitals across India a reality.

Bansal elaborated further, a pilot project can be started in one of the states, say, Tamil Nadu.

Tamil Nadu, a large state with a large population decides to develop Coimbatore as it's Tool-room Capital. The state will facilitate the process of earmarking land for such an activity. Having earmarked the land, the state would have to develop that land by building all necessary services such as water availability, electricity, waste collection centers, roads, in-land port or seaport, etc. The development of all these services takes time and resources. Only a state government can provide that. Having developed the services for Tool-room activities, the land can be divided into smaller plots.

Sumit added, exactly, the plots can be of different sizes ranging from 200 square meters to 2000 square meters. These plots can then be sold to potential Tool-room Operators with the objective of creating a Tool-room hub.

To which, I said, yes, and existing Tool-room Operators such as Daler across the state shall be encouraged to shift to the new Tool-room hub.

Bansal asked Daler, Bhai, will you shift to a new Tool-room hub if there is one?

Daler said, why not.

I continued, besides encouraging existing Tool-room operators across the state, new entrepreneurs shall also be encouraged to set-up Tool-rooms.

Yea, Bansal further added, the objective of the state government shall not be profit-making from the sale of such plots. Instead, the focus should be on developing a world-class Tool-room hub. Sumit said, true, serious entrepreneurs with a real passion for Tool-room shall be encouraged. The plots can be sold or leased.

I said leasing is a better option as this will not only encourage startup entrepreneurs with very little capital to set-up Tool-rooms but also eliminate land aggregators.

Since I had developed good marketing acumen, I further added, the land leasing activity shall be promoted across the whole state on a variety of platforms including traditional media as well as online media.

Sumit said I think, this is the need of the hour. He stressed that the state government will need to allocate resources for the creation of Tool-room Capital.

Bansal said, yea, this is doable by Minister-in-charge. The Minister-in-charge must make sure to include startup entrepreneurs in the formal policymaking role as well.

Bansal continued, good, having earmarked the State's Tool-room capital and having developed the land for that Tool-room Capital, the Minister-in-charge shall now encourage existing as well as potential Tool-room operators to shift to this new Tool-room capital in the state.

I added, exactly, the leasing terms shall be attractive for Tool-room operators to shift to this new Tool-room capital. Besides the attractive land leasing terms, the electricity, water shall be provided at subsidized rates. When we as a nation can provide subsidized electricity and water to farmers, what stops the state governments across India to provide electricity, water at subsidized rates to Tool-room operators?

To which Daler replied, sir Jee, why are you showing me a dream?

We just smiled.

However, Bansal continued, if we as a nation want to reduce the trade deficit with China, if we as a nation want to promote bottom-up manufacturing, if we as a nation want to manufacture everyday simple household goods such as Chappal, Agarbatti, toys in India, then, surely, we need to support the bottom-up manufacturing.

Sumit then said this is a massive idea. Tool-room capitals across states in India. Wow, this is truly a massive idea. However, large scale infrastructure would need to be developed for implementing this kind of idea. Besides the attractive land lease terms, subsidized electricity and water, the other infrastructure such as roads, the in-land port shall be developed on a war footing to facilitate the movement of goods from this Tool-room capital.

Bansal's eyes were glittering. A manufacturing entrepreneur such as our Sumit with an idea in mind to develop new toys, agarbatti, chappals, electrical products, auto products, daily household products would simply visit this Tool-room capital and get his/her mold done there.

I said, true, this entrepreneur can get a quote from various Tool-room operators in the Tool-room capital. And based on his/her judgment, this entrepreneur can choose the best Tool-room operator to develop his/her mold.

Bansal further added, in addition to getting the mold ready, this entrepreneur would manufacture the first 500 or 1000 pieces of that product in the Tool-room capital and thereafter assemble & package the finished pieces and would simply start selling.

I said, fabulous - if the product does well, then, there it is, an idea has become a thriving business. An idea has become a thriving business within a span of 3 months. If the entrepreneur is unable to sell his/her product, then, at least, he or she got the failure certificate in 3 months and not in 1 year. That's such a relief.

Sumit couldn't hide his excitement. I would have jumped into entrepreneurship if something like this was available. However, there would still be challenges in scaling up. Manufacturing and selling 500-1000 pieces is one thing, but building a sustainable business is another thing altogether.

I said, true, I am experiencing it at this stage. Venture capital funds are not bullish on investing in a manufacturing start-up because they see a plethora of government-business touchpoints. They all are happy investing in internet-based businesses.

Chapter 9.3

Reason Number 3: Lack of common mechanism to obtain various approvals for scaling up the business

Bansal nodded in agreement with me. Yea, scaling up is an issue. Big issue! Even after being in the manufacturing business for over a decade, I still face all these challenges. It still takes a hell of a lot of time to obtain so many approvals.

I said, first of all, let us think ahead. Who is going to be a manufacturing entrepreneur in the future?

Sumit added, certainly not people who are already 50 or above. New-age entrepreneurs who are going to be involved in manufacturing in India are the people currently in the age group of 25 - 40. Just like all of us sitting here.

I said true, new-age manufacturing entrepreneurs in the age group of 25 - 40 are all used to a certain degree of services. Services like applying for a passport, housing, shopping, ticket booking, etc. This age group is used to the services on their smartphone. No one wants to visit the 'Sarkari Daftar' or 'Government office' to apply for a passport, license, electricity connection, or water connection. Things are done online. Documents are submitted online. Appointments are taken online.

Bansal and Daler simply nodded in agreement. Daler said, most of the people who come to me for mold development are in the 20s or 30s.

I continued, yea, this new age group has also moved out from traditional plotted housing to apartments in group housing societies. This age group is used to services at their doorsteps. Therefore, questions that policymakers shall ask are the following:

- Why the hell this new age manufacturing entrepreneur is going to visit a government office to obtain different approvals?
- Won't it deter this new age group from entering the manufacturing sector in the first place?
- Won't this new age group simply end up becoming a trader and will source goods from China and sell in India?
- Won't this new age group rather join the Tech sector?

Bansal said, true, Sachin Bhai, if our policymakers ask these questions, then, it is inevitable that they would make policies that encourage new-age entrepreneurs to become real manufacturing entrepreneurs and manufacture world-class products in India thereby increasing the nation's income as well as generating millions of manufacturing jobs.

Sumit said, as I see the manufacturing business from outside, besides the creation of Tool-room capitals across states in India, the policymakers should also focus on the process of scaling up a manufacturing business. The goal should be to make scaling up as easy as possible. And granting faster approvals shall be the goal.

I said, true. I continued, Sumit, you had this idea to develop a toy airplane. You couldn't find that kind of design in the marketplace. You aren't manufacturing it because of obstacles that you foresee in developing the molds. You know that mold making is going to take a good 8-9 months. And you simply do not have this much time given the fact that you are already settled in a public sector job. However, if it only took 1-2 months to develop the molds, then, surely, you would have given it a shot.

Bansal said, of course, anyone would give it a shot. The fear of failure will subside.

Sumit, yea, I would have considered it.

Exactly, I said, let us now suppose that policymakers do rectify this issue by developing Tool-room capitals across states in India and mold making becomes faster in India. Let us now suppose it takes just about 45 days to make a mold in India. Now, Sumit would be tempted to develop this toy airplane. Sumit would be tempted to sit with designers such as Daler to first develop the design and then develop the molds. Once molds are ready and the prototype is as per the Sumit's imagination, then, Sumit would manufacture the first set of 500 or 1000 pieces in a Tool-room capital. Thereafter, Sumit would spend his energies on marketing & selling by leveraging online as well as offline channels. Based on the feedback on this first set of 500 or 1000 toy airplanes, Sumit now decides to get into the manufacturing at a larger scale.

Bansal added, to manufacture on a large scale, he would have to quit his job.

I said, true, however, he knows, molds are ready and the supply chain is all sorted out and marketing channels are fine-tuned as well. All looks under control.

Daler quipped, however, to start manufacturing on a larger scale, Sumit Bhai would have to set-up a manufacturing facility. And setting up a manufacturing facility takes a long long time.

I said, exactly, to set-up a manufacturing facility, Sumit would need faster access to services. Otherwise, he would not jump into the manufacturing business by leaving his stable job.

Sumit nodded in agreement, yea, services such as electricity connection, water connection, layout plan, firefighting license, environmental clearance, etc. shall be provided to me in quick time to keep the momentum going.

Daler said, how is it possible? Given the current processes, Sumit Bhai would have to apply for each & every service individually and that sure would take a hell of a lot of time.

I said I know, this could take a good 6-8 months as was highlighted by one investor, Manoj - when he narrated the story of his manufacturing friend.

Bansal said, I know it as well, it's a tedious job. However, how can it be simplified not just for Sumit, but for myself, yourself, as well as for many other new-age manufacturing entrepreneurs?

I responded we and many of the new-age entrepreneurs are used to living in group housing societies wherein all we have to do is 'rent' or 'buy' a housing unit or an apartment in these housing societies and simply start living. There is no pillar to pillar run for getting individual water connection, individual electricity connection, layout approval, occupancy certificate, completion certificate.

Sumit said, 100%, I remember when one of my uncles (Chacha) developed his plotted house in Faridabad. He had to run from one government office to another to obtain a water connection, electricity connection, map approval, occupancy certificate, and a completion certificate. That whole process was tedious and of course, his architect did manage all of these activities but not without paying the officers.

Bansal said, oh, I have to do this not just for my own house, but also for setting up the Mangolpuri plant. It's truly tedious and time-consuming.

I continued, exactly, Sumit and people like us who are used to living in an apartment in a group housing society would find all these tasks rather unnecessary. Therefore, we would prefer something on similar lines. In other words, we would prefer to start this manufacturing journey in a manufacturing society.

Daler said you are coming up with new terminologies.

I said, yes, a manufacturing society. A manufacturing society is developed along the lines of a housing society. Just like in a housing society, wherein one simply 'rents' or 'buys' the apartment and starts living, similarly, a manufacturing society would be a place or set-up wherein one simply 'rents' or 'buys' space and starts manufacturing. Just like in a housing society, services are provided by a common authority (builder or a facility management team), likewise, in a manufacturing society, services shall be provided by a common authority. Sumit and many of us new-age manufacturing entrepreneurs won't have to go through the maze of obtaining various approvals in the manufacturing sector in India.

Bansal said, but, how would the structure of this manufacturing society look like?

I explained, just like, a housing society has thousands of apartments, a manufacturing society would have thousands of spaces, small or large, in order to start manufacturing in a quick time period. This manufacturing society would be managed by a common authority. A common private authority. Space owners in this manufacturing society can hire a common authority or service provider say a private company like GMR. This common authority will be paid monthly on a pro-rata basis for the services it renders to space owners. Water connection, electricity connection, drainage management, power back-up, maintenance, common water treatment plant, security, firefighting services, other services will be provided by this common authority.

Sumit then added, great, just like a 'resident welfare association' in a housing society can change the facility management company, likewise, the 'space owners association' in this manufacturing society can change the common authority and hire a new company to manage the services.

Daler seemed excited and asked, what will policymakers need to do to facilitate this kind of manufacturing society?

I said the government or policymakers have to draft an act, a manufacturing act, much like they have drafted the apartment act. Under this manufacturing act, the space owners association would have the statutory rights to govern the whole manufacturing society.

Sumit was excited too, I like it, a manufacturing entrepreneur would simply 'rent' or 'buy' space in this manufacturing society and abide by the rules set by the manufacturing society.

I said, yea, an entrepreneur would pay for services based on consumption. There are no freebies, but setting up a manufacturing business will become rather easy. An entrepreneur wouldn't have to run pillar to pillar for approvals. The manufacturing society would have all the necessary approvals and would simply provide services to the entrepreneur.

Bansal said, I think, you have thought through this.

I said, yea, I have been meeting various investors to invest in my company and they all are hesitant investing in manufacturing start-up because of government-business touchpoints.

Bansal then added, great, I wish, this kind of manufacturing society was available to me as well.

I said, this concept of manufacturing societies can't be restricted to new manufacturing societies alone, in fact, old manufacturing parks or industrial areas can be covered in this manufacturing society act. Each and every existing manufacturing park or industrial area can form its own 'space owners association' and hire a private common company that can deliver common services.

Bansal said, sounds solid Bhai, now, Sumit, who decides to scale up his toy airplane business, would simply 'rent' space in one of the existing manufacturing parks or industrial areas and start manufacturing without having to run from one government office to another for approvals.

I said, exactly, the common authority will manage all these tasks. Sumit would just bring in the machines and equipment to start manufacturing.

Bansal said I agree, besides improving the 'ease of doing business' for manufacturing entrepreneurs, these manufacturing societies will help in reducing operating costs. I can speak from my own experience. In our manufacturing set-up in Nangloi and Mangolpuri Industrial area. We have installed our own power back-up systems, cooling towers, water treatment plants, waste management systems. Firstly, installing all these systems incurred a huge amount of capital expenditure. Secondly, managing these systems on a regular basis incur an operating cost no matter if these systems are used partially.

Therein lies the advantage that a manufacturing society can provide. If my manufacturing plants were part of the manufacturing society, then, I wouldn't have to invest in unnecessary water treatment, power back-up, cooling towers, waste management systems. I would simply take services provided by the common authority and pay as per the usage.

I said, exactly Bansal Bhai, besides savings on the capital expenditure front, you would now deploy all of your resources in the actual manufacturing of finished products. There would be a peace of mind as far as availing other services are concerned.

Bansal said, clearly, I remember one day when power had been cut in our Mangolpuri plant and the plant supervisor Kishan turned his attention to start the power back-up generator. The generator did not start, and a mechanic had to be called on to repair the generator. It took a good 3 hours. During those 3 hours, there was no work. Loss of productivity as well as money.

I said, yes, with a manufacturing society, such issues can be avoided. Productivity will improve while operating costs will come down. The final products will be more competitive in the marketplace. Economies of scale can be achieved. A manufacturing society will be able to help in achieving economies of scale that in turn will make India's products globally competitive.

Bansal said I would surely appreciate such a concept wherein facilities can be shared. Sumit said yea and future entrepreneurs such as myself would surely appreciate these common services provided by the common authority in a manufacturing society. I am already able to relate to this. I have seen it in my own housing society wherein power back-up, water management, drainage management, waste management activities are provided by the facility management company. I didn't have to install my own power

back-up (inverter), water tank, drainage, etc. However, if I was living in a plotted house,

I would have to install all these systems for my home. So many savings on the capital

expenditure front. And moreover, the cost of maintaining these systems is shared

among all the apartment owners in a group housing society.

Daler too nodded in agreement. I can imagine the benefits this kind of structure would

bring to Indian manufacturing entrepreneurs. The benefits could be so massive that we

can't even imagine at this stage. The benefits would surely make Indian manufacturing

globally competitive.

I said, bang on, we don't have the exact numbers on possible savings. But interest

costs on Capex as well as maintenance costs on individual systems (water

management, power back-up, water treatment, waste management, drainage system)

will far outnumber the monthly charges paid to the common authority in a manufacturing

society.

Bansal further added, apart from making Indian manufacturing globally competitive, the

concept of manufacturing society can also result in protecting the environment.

Environment? I looked at Bansal and asked, what? how?

Bansal started to explain that since services will be shared, there will be less wastage.

Power wastage, water wastage will be eliminated. Generators are one of the biggest

causes of pollution in our cities. And when manufacturing companies start using the

power back-up provided by common authority, then, need for individual generators will

disappear. That will surely be a big tick in tackling air pollution in Indian cities. Moreover,

waste management will become truly top class.

Sumit said, hmmm - while visiting a typical manufacturing area or industrial area, we all see heaps of waste on the streets. The whole area looks unhygienic. However, people get used to it thinking that it's the norm in a typical industrial area.

Bansal responded it happens because an entrepreneur is focused on reducing costs and managing waste at an individual level becomes too costly. Therefore, there is no commitment to practice environment-friendly policies. The government of the day clearly sets the environmental guidelines, however, all these guidelines are overlooked under cost pressures.

I said, with a manufacturing society structure, the waste management guidelines will be followed and cost would be shared among all space owners.

I also narrated my meeting with venture capital investor - Manoj - to Sumit, Daler, and Bansal. I said Manoj wasn't too keen on investing in a manufacturing business because of the time it takes to set the ball in motion. He wasn't enthused with a plethora of government-business touchpoints. Maybe with the adoption of manufacturing society structure resulting in negligible government-business touchpoints, venture capital funds may get more optimistic about investing in manufacturing start-ups. Truth be told, India needs millions of manufacturing companies. These companies will first help in narrowing down the trade deficit with China and then expand Indian exports.

Bansal said, exactly, an entrepreneur can nurture an idea up to a certain stage. Post that, capital is needed to scale up operations. Government schemes can't be the solution.

I said, true, unless and until venture capital firms come in and invest in Indian manufacturing space the way they invest in Indian Tech space, we can't reduce our trade deficit with China. We can't create millions of manufacturing jobs. Therefore, the government-business touchpoints need to be reduced in a manufacturing business. Daler too was excited by this discussion, so true, the manufacturing society concept can certainly be a step in this direction. However, don't forget the cost of financing, it's way too expensive, at least for tool-room operators like myself.

Chapter 9.4

Reason Number 4: Lack of financial support for Tool-room operators across India

Before Daler could say anything on the cost of financing, Bansal picked it up, Yea, the cost of financing is too high.

Bansal said, 'Sachin you are lucky that your first set of molds have been completed in 8 months' time period. He explained to me that Tool-room operators, not just Daler but most of them would simply keep on taking orders from various entrepreneurs despite knowing fully well that they won't be able to deliver the molds on time.

I asked Daler, why do you do this?

To which, Daler replied, 'Money'. I asked, 'Money'? How? Explain to me in detail.

Daler explained to me that we buy CNC machines from overseas such as from Taipei, Taiwan, and bring those machines to India. As you can see even in this expo, I am considering buying a Chinese machine. All of it costs a huge amount of money, sometimes upwards of Rupees 50 Lacs. I have 4 such CNC machines. And I recently bought one from Taiwan. And since not just me but most tool-room operators would not have access to funds, therefore, we take a loan from banks. And interest rates on these commercial loans are about 15%. 15% for those who have borrowed in the past and have a good credit history. If someone is a newcomer, then, interest rates on such loans would be close to 18%. So, when we buy CNC machines, we are liable to pay monthly installments to banks. And that means, we simply start taking on orders from entrepreneurs to manage our cash flow and pay the monthly installments as well as manage other expenses.

'Bansal' further added that Daler has secured about 80% of the mold cost from him within a period of 2 months. And Daler would deliver that mold in 8-10 months' time. This way, Daler is safe and secure. I know it, and Daler knows it too.

Daler was honest, this way, I, as well as other tool-room operators, manage our monthly liabilities.

Bansal taunted Daler, saying that 'they all are the same'. If you had gone to some other Tool-room operator, then, I am telling you Sachin, you would be literally crying. Literally crying.

I understood what Daler meant by money. I also understood the limitations of Daler to deliver the mold on time. I knew that the whole manufacturing policy (especially bottom-up manufacturing) needs to be looked at comprehensively.

I said It is clear that the Tool-room operators require some sort of financial support to buy CNC machines. Financial support that encourages them to install more CNC machines to fulfill the mold development orders that they take from entrepreneurs.

Sumit said, there are so many financial schemes these days. Can central or state governments support Tool-room operators financially by providing interest subsidy to purchase CNC machines?

I said, yes, the answer is 'Yes'. I was reading about the central government's one of the most talked-about schemes MUDRA. 'Micro Units Development and Refinance Agency

Bank is a public sector financial institution in India. It provides loans at low rates to micro-finance institutions and non-banking financial institutions which then provide credit to MSMEs. There are 3 kinds of loans that are provided to the needy. Shishu, Kishore, and Tarun. Under Shishu, loans up to Rs 50000 are granted. Under Kishore, loans from Rs 50000 to Rs 500000 are provided. Under Tarun, loans from Rs 500000 to Rs 1000000 are provided. I showed them the data from the last 3 years:

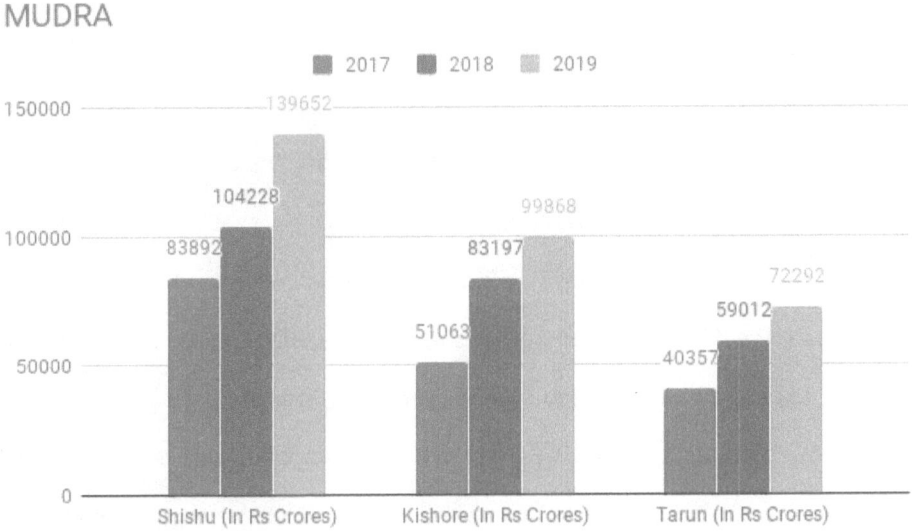

The data for MUDRA loan has been obtained from RBI[2]

I continued, of the 3 kinds of loans disbursed under the MUDRA scheme, Shishu (loan value up to Rs 50000) has been disbursed more in each of the 3 years. The total amount disbursed under the Shishu loan is Rs 327772 Crores in the years 2017, 2018,

[2] https://timesofindia.indiatimes.com/business/india-business/watch-out-for-rising-bad-loans-under-mudra-scheme-rbi/articleshow/72249235.cms

and 2019. Many economists, as well as commentators, are of the view that Shishu loan does not go into income-generating activities and instead ends up becoming a consumption loan. Therefore, there are concerns that NPA (Non-Performing Asset) may rise especially in the Shishu loan. In the fiscal year 2017-18, the NPAs were 2.52%. Whereas NPAs increased to 2.68% in 2018-19.

It is clearly visible from the data above that Rs 327772 Crores granted under the Shishu loan may end up becoming a consumption loan. Will it increase people's income? Will it increase the nation's income? The answer is No.

Daler added this is a huge amount of money. Why don't they bring in such schemes for tool-room operators or for the manufacturing sector?

Bansal said, true, instead, this money (Rs 327772 Crores) could have been better utilized to support the 'Make in India' program, especially the bottom-up manufacturing to lend money to people like Daler and other Tool-room operators.

Daler nodded in agreement, yes, I, as well as, other Tool-room operators with access to subsidized funds would buy more CNC machines. In other words, we would build our capacity to fulfill the mold development orders that we take from entrepreneurs like Sachin Bhai and Bansal Jee. The end result would be the completion of molds in a set time period of 1 - 2 months. At the same time, to fulfill mold development orders on time, we would employ more people, thereby generating employment under the 'Make in India' program.

Bansal added, exactly, when molds are developed on time, an entrepreneur will be able to launch his/her product in a quick time and assess the feedback on his/her product. If feedback is positive, then, the entrepreneur can convert the idea or product into a thriving business. If feedback is not encouraging, then, the entrepreneur can modify the mold or abandon the project. But the entrepreneur will be able to take action within a span of 3 months and not wait till 1 year.

I said, so true, people like Sumit would also jump into entrepreneurship. The bottom-up manufacturing would result in an increase in people's income as well as the nation's income. The bottom-up manufacturing would result in a reduction in trade deficit with China. The bottom-up manufacturing would result in a boost in Indian exports.

Daler said the cost of financing must surely come down if the government is serious about the 'Make in India' program. If funds under the Shishu loan category can't be touched for any other activity, then, surely, it's high time the central government, as well as state governments, must allocate funds for the development of Tool-room capitals across each and every Indian state. At the same time, people like us, the Tool-room operators, must be financially supported to build the capacity, to purchase new CNC machines. So that we can fulfill our commitments on time and help people like you in launching new products at a faster pace.

I added, therefore, the policymakers shall constantly ask this question, whether the support that the state or central government provides increases people's income or not? If the answer is 'No', then, the financial support must go to programs that increase people's income. Investment in 'Make in India' is a policy decision that will increase people's income.

Sumit interrupted me, what do you mean by an increase in people's income?

I said, hmmm, it can be understood better by analyzing a typical lower-middle-class household in India. A typical lower-middle-class household in India is always grappling with the issue of spending. The income is already low and therefore every month is spent worrying about household expenditure. How much to spend on food, how much to spend on housing, how much to spend on electricity, transport, health, etc. And how much to spend on kids' education, how much to spend on coaching classes for kids, how much to spend on nutrition, etc. One set of spending comes under the category of 'consumption expenditure', while another set of spending comes under the category of 'productive expenditure'.

Sumit said, yea, true.

I continued, consumption expenditures such as food, housing, electricity, transport, clothing are needed to survive. Therefore, spending on these consumption expenditures is always required. There is no way a typical lower-middle-class household can get around this expenditure. On the other hand, Productive expenditures such as education, coaching, training, nutrition take a cut. A typical lower-middle-class household has no other option but to cut the spendings on Productive expenditure. However, it is also true, if a typical lower-middle-class household does not increase its spendings on productive expenditure, then, how can this household expect its income to increase in the future?

Everyone nodded in agreement.

I said, by spending on productive expenditures such as quality education, the household enhances its capacity to increase its household income in the future. Whereas if this household continues to spend all its current income on Consumption expenditure, then, this household can not expect its income to increase in the future and thereby this household remains in that lower-middle-income trap.

Bansal said got it, this is also true of India. India like any other country generates its income by taxing (direct as well as indirect). These resources are spent on the country's consumption expenditures and productive expenditures.

I said yea, all spending on subsidies, paying salaries, maintenance, freebies, loan waivers, free cylinder, free electricity comes under the category of consumption expenditures. All spending on building new infrastructure, building new factories, educational institutes, schools comes under the category of productive expenditures. India continues to spend the majority of its resources on consumption expenditures. However, some percentage is still spent on productive expenditures. I don't have exact numbers.

Sumit said, yea, in the past, because of high levels of corruption, the consumption expenditures partially reached the actual beneficiary. Rajiv Gandhi once famously said that of the Rupee 1 spent, only 15 Paise reached the actual beneficiary.

I added, things have improved because of technology. JAM (Jan Dhan, Aadhar, and Mobile) has reduced the leakages in the system. Spending meant for consumption expenditure is going to the actual beneficiary. The role of Babus has reduced. However, when it comes to Productive expenditures, the Babus still frame and implement the policies.

Bansal added, let's not take that route. We have already discussed it on that get-together.

I said, yea, therefore, the respective Minister-in-charge shall make a committee of real people and spend the nation's money wisely in order to increase the nation's future income. The Information Technology sector had no Babus and not even a minister at that time and still increased the nation's income manifold in 20-30 years. The manufacturing sector can and shall increase the nation's income. It can become a productive sector provided startup entrepreneurs are included in the process of policymaking.

Bansal said, so true, and when we talk about investment in the 'Make in India' program, we talk about investment in bottom-up manufacturing. Again, it appears, real entrepreneurs are not involved in the development of such policies.

Bansal then got a call from his Mangolpuri plant. He became animated over the call that lasted for about 10 minutes or so. The expo was closing as well by that time. It was already 6 PM. Sumit and I were delighted with the kinds of machines we were able to see at the expo. Daler felt satisfied. He had identified a polishing machine. Bansal was happy too until that call.

I asked him, what happened Bansal Bhai? All well?

Bansal said, yea, all is well, just some labor issues at the plant. It's a daily problem.

Chapter 9.5

Reason Number 5: Lack of skilled labor

Daler too joined in, yea, it's a daily issue. Not only it is difficult to find trained labor but also it is difficult to constantly upgrade their skills including communication skills. It's a massive challenge for Tool-room operators as well as manufacturing companies.

Yea, I said, Daler Jee, during my visits to your Tool-room, I interacted with people working there. Some of them are new and some are working for you for the last 4-5 years. I asked some of them about their past working experiences. And none of them had working experiences in mold development or any other manufacturing set-up. Neither did they undergo any formal training in mold development or manufacturing processes.

Daler smiled and said, yea, they all learned on the job. Which is not a bad thing. But I accept upgrading their skills is a huge challenge.

To which Bansal said, however, on the job learning is good when attention is paid to the processes, quality, and timely delivery.

But, I said, there was none of that at Daler's Tool-room. People worked in a haphazard way. There was no checklist of things to do. People will work on the mold and forget to polish certain parts. The mold will be delivered without polishing certain parts. And during trials, the mold would give errors resulting in the waste of raw material as well as time. Then, the mold will return to Daler's Tool-room again, polishing will be done. This whole process will repeat 3-4 times before the mold is finally ready.

Bansal said yea, the whole process of transporting, trials, loading/unloading would take an enormous amount of time, thereby increasing the cost of development of the mold and at the same time decreasing the quality of the mold. When mold quality has deteriorated during this whole process, the final manufactured goods produced would be of lesser quality.

I said, with these lesser quality goods, how can Indian manufacturing compete with Chinese manufacturing? We are again talking about bottom-up manufacturing. In top-down manufacturing, large enterprises such as Maruti, Samsung, LG have access to funds and they develop their own Tool-rooms. However, in bottom-up manufacturing, all an entrepreneur has is just an idea. An idea to manufacture simple daily-use household goods such as toys, agarbatti, electrical products, consumer products, disposable items, etc. Therefore, an entrepreneur needs access to high quality yet affordable Tool-rooms.

Daler added I agree, an entrepreneur requires access to high-quality Tool-room. A Tool-room where the trained staff is able to carry out mold development tasks in a timely and qualitative manner. And to achieve that, the Tool-room operator needs skilled people. That's why I say, manpower is a big challenge for all of us.

Sumit though added, the government of India has launched a skill development program. How is it working on the ground?

I said, maybe, the need of the hour is to double or triple down the focus on creating skilled people for the mold development tasks as well as other manufacturing tasks.

Daler added these tasks would include welding, polishing, machining, operating CNC machines, cutting, loading/unloading, preparing a quality checklist, drilling, assembling, packaging, etc.

Bansal said, trained people on these sets of activities will be able to produce high-quality molds, thereby encouraging entrepreneurs to make high-quality products resulting in a boom in Indian manufacturing. Trained people will also be able to enhance the productivity of the entire manufacturing set-up thereby making Indian manufacturing globally competitive.

Bansal again highlighted the success of Chinese manufacturing. It is very well documented that college-educated personnel is 3 times more productive than less than 10th grade educated personnel. Chinese leadership focused on this aspect to grow fast economically as well as to enhance their manufacturing productivity. And since 1998, the enrollment in college education rose phenomenally. The investment China made in the 1990s and still continues to do so in college education as well as in skill development programs had paid massive dividends. Not only has China become the world's factory but it also has grown phenomenally in economic terms. As things stand today, the Chinese economy is 4.5 times the Indian economy in nominal terms.

True, Sumit said, the impact of education and skill development is not limited to the enhanced productivity of an individual. In fact, US economist Edwin Mansfield in his 1971 study found that the presidents and managers of companies that have been early adopters of the technology were much younger and more educated than presidents or managers of firms that were slow adopters of technology. There is a strong correlation between skilled/educated workforce and productivity.

Right, I said, and productivity just doesn't mean getting things done fast. It also means getting things done fast in a qualitative manner.

Bansal then quoted, Tim Cook, Apple CEO, he once said that popular perception that companies come to China because of low labor costs is a myth. Rather companies come to China because labor is highly skilled.

However, I said, from my own experience so far in developing the molds, manufacturing of front cover as well as the back cover, I would testify to the fact that labor in India is not properly trained to perform manufacturing tasks.

Exactly, Bansal replied, even in my company, I am always struggling with trained staff. Large corporations such as Maruti, Samsung, LG (Top-down manufacturing) would obviously be able to attract skilled labor and these corporations would also be able to further train the labor to become more competitive. However, we (bottom-up manufacturing) need access to a wider pool of skilled labor. In this context, only the governments, states or central, have the wherewithal to equip the people with necessary skills & education.

I added, besides the government focused programs on skill development, the industry bodies can play an important role as well. I clearly remember from my own experience at a software company. They gave a massive importance to 'training'. My company as well as industry body NASSCOM had developed high-quality training modules for workers at different levels. Manufacturing industry bodies must take a leaf out of NASSCOM's commitment to continuous training programs in order to upgrade the workers on an ongoing basis. Manufacturing industry bodies must develop training curricula in order to upgrade the workers on an ongoing basis. Besides the technical skills, the people in the sales department shall be trained as well. From my own interactions with salespeople of many manufacturing companies, I came to realize that these people lack soft skills. Soft skills such as proper communication, politeness, discipline. All of these skills are very much needed for a manufacturing company aiming to sell products in Indian as well as global markets.

Everyone simply concurred with me. We all were debating and discussing issues plaguing the manufacturing sector from our own experiences. There was no intellectual or bookish debate. Rather, it was all experiential.

Chapter 10

Finally

"If you can't give them bread, give them opium" was the famous saying during the roman empire. India shall not subscribe to this statement. However, given our population size, the need to focus on manufacturing is paramount to give people the bread that they seek. Or else, we as a nation would be taking our people on the path towards opium.

Let's understand this from simple calculations.

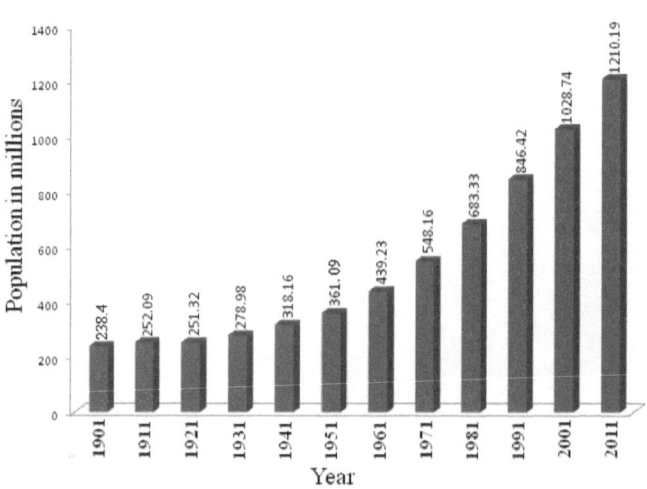

As per the census report of 1981, the Indian population was 683.33 million. The population increased to 846.42 million in 1991. And as per the 2001 census, the Indian population was 1028.74 million. In other words, India added 163.09 million people from 1981 to 1991 and 182.32 million people from 1991 to 2001. Therefore, the total number of people added between 1981 and 2001 was 345.41 million.

Now, these people will form the working-age group in 2021. In other words, 345.41 million people shall ideally become part of the workforce by 2021 when their age will be in the most productive working age of 20 - 40. There is no formal data on employment. However, many of these 345.41 million people would end up working in the farm sector, many in the informal sector and some percentage in the formal sector. There are concerns about unemployment rates in India. As per the government's own reports, there were 31 million jobless people as of September 2018. These numbers are widely disputed though.

However, the demographic dividend that we kept hearing from time to time can turn into a demographic disaster that feeds off of opium such as the ideological debates that we keep witnessing in our country. Ideological debates such as the Patidar movement in Gujarat, JAT agitations in Rajasthan, Jallikattu in Tamil Nadu are some of the ideological debates that jobless people feed off on. In other words, the roman empire's saying 'when you can't give them bread, give them opium' appears to be becoming a reality. And our intellectual media, historians with bread on their plate don't mind spreading the opium called ideological debates among the jobless youth.

The discourse on social media platforms including on WhatsApp, Facebook, Twitter is mostly about these ideological debates rather than on sorting out the manufacturing mess. Unless we as a society are able to frame policies that encourage manufacturing and provide millions of jobs to people, we will continue to have these ideological debates one after the other.

The discourse among people shall be towards bread and not towards opium. Whenever there is an India-China tension of any kind, the discourse on social media platforms shifts towards criticizing traders, business people who source goods from China. In doing so, the discourse certainly shifts to the wrong side of the pendulum. Instead, the discourse shall be directed towards generating momentum to raise people's income. The manufacturing sector has the potential to do so. Therefore, the discourse on social media shall shift towards manufacturing policy framework. The discourse shall shift towards questions such as 'Why are traders/businessmen sourcing goods from China?', 'Why aren't Indian manufacturers manufacturing in India?'. When these sets of questions become part of the discourse, then, certainly the discourse will shift towards the right side of the pendulum.

The society, as well as start-up entrepreneurs, can put pressure on the government of the day to boost the manufacturing sector in India. By involving real people in policy-making, by creating Tool-room capitals across states in India, by adopting the concept of 'manufacturing society', by easing the financing norms for Tool-room operators, and by doubling the focus on skill development programs, India can achieve the necessary growth in the manufacturing sector. India can neutralize its trade deficit with China. India can have surplus trade with other world economies. India can create Crores of manufacturing jobs.